AA'S
12 STEPS
FOR EVERYONE

The Key To Being Recovered

Volume III

Sponsorship 101

TIP #1: HOW TO IDENTIFY A NEWCOMER

"WHAT ! ! ! "

"An order?"

"I can't go through with it!"

Other Books by SantaC

AA's
12 STEPS
FOR
EVERYONE
The KEY To Being Recovery

Volume I
12 Steps for the Spiritually Challenged

Volume II
Prayer and Meditation

For information about bulk purchase discounts please contact:

info@SantasKey2Recovery.com

Website & E-Books Purchase:

http://www.SantasKey2Recovery.com

AA's

12 STEPS
FOR EVERYONE
The Key To Being Recovered

Volume III

Sponsorship 101
How to be a Successful Sponsor Every Time

By SantaC

© SantaC 2012. Except as provided by the copyright Act (Title 17 US Code) no part of this publication may be reproduced, stored in a retrieval system or transmitted in any form or by any means without the prior written permission of the publisher.

1stPrinting 2012

Library of Congress

Registration Number: pending

Effective date of registration:

September 15, 2012

ISBN: 978-1477452462

FORWARD

SantaC's book, 'AA's 12 Steps for Everyone - The Key to Being Recovered' contains the truth about A.A., Sponsorship and will give you the Key to Being Recovered. Read this book and find out how they had a 93% recovery rate in Cleveland in the early 1940s and how you can apply the same principles applied then, today.

This book shows you how to qualify a sponsee and using the same principles how to find a good sponsor. You will learn how to sponsor new A.A.'s and give them the key to being recovered. From this book you will meet your Higher Power and see God, the same as I and many others have.

Gary G.

Table of Contents

Introduction	1
In The Beginning	4
The Tent Is Too Small For The Circus	5
Many Roads to Hell Are Paved With Good Intentions	8
The Traditions In A Nutshell	13
The 12 Steps In Plain English	14
Unity	15
Discussion Topic: Back To Basics	17
God Shots	23
AA Sponsorship Pamphlet	24
Ways To Stop Drinking	37
What Is A Sponsor	52
And As Dr. Bob Reported	56
What Was Early A.A. Really Like?	59
A Manual For Alcoholics Anonymous	71
The Specifics Of What The Founders Did In Akron	118
What Does A Sponsor Do?	119
Approaching The Newcomer	123
The Ability to Listen Correctly	132
Going Through The Steps With A Sponsee	133
Sponsorship	147

Untreated Alcoholism – Who Me?	149
Dr. Bob's Prescription For Sobriety	152
I've Never Quit Being Active	153
The Prescription	157

APPENDICES

Appendix I – The Steps OF A.A. – An Interpretation	160
Appendix II – That Ain't In The Book	172
Appendix III – Memo From GOD	199

Bibliography	204

The publication of this volume does not imply affiliation with, nor approval or endorsement from Alcoholics Anonymous World Services, Inc. The views expressed herein are solely those of the author. A.A. is a program of recovery from alcoholism. The Twelve Steps are used in connection with programs and activities which are patterned after A.A. but address other issues, does not imply otherwise

Working with others is the annuity in the program of being **Recovered**. For those of you who don't know, an annuity is a paid up life insurance policy that pays you dividends on a regular basis.

Working with others is a High that cannot be explained; it has to be felt! When someone you are working with **gets it**…

This is when you get to see God. When someone you've worked with is working with a newcomer and that newcomer gets **It !!!** It is a natural High that cannot be duplicated or explained…

This is the foundation of A.A.; Working With Others.
The Alpha and the Omega.

This book is dedicated to my first sponsors Cathy S., Harry L., Mel C., and my current sponsor Jay P. who I've had for 20 years and the many people that trusted me to be their sponsor and share the innermost secrets of their lives.

Thank You

SantaC

INTRODUCTION

It is my intention to demystify this business of Sponsorship. To explain what the responsibilities are and the accountability that goes with being one.

There is great responsibility in that you will have the life of an individual in your hands. If done properly you will develop a long and lasting friendship in addition to saving a life and helping to repair the relationships on many levels of the newcomer's life.

It is in practicing the 12 steps in all of my affairs, so that I will become a beckon of light for others to see. As the old Spiritual says; "I once was lost, but now I am found." I have become happy, joyous and free, usefully whole and a productive member of society. You too may possess this.

Now when I first read the 12 steps and listened to those who were in my early meetings, I thought to myself this isn't going to work. This is too simple and besides they don't know the trouble I'm in or the problems that I have.

My wife was leaving for the second time. Oh, and she was my second wife. I was in the U.S. Navy and my performance at work was beginning to be questioned. Yada yada yada….you can fill in the blanks….from your own story. I am more interested in the Solution and not how you or I got here. I am going to present some history from various sources so you will have an idea on what it was like, what they did and what they were like when they finished doing the work.

It is my intention to acknowledge all sources and where that information was obtained. If I leave anybody out, Please Forgive me, it was not intentional.

I am really old school, so I am sure to ruffle some feathers. So be it. I am told the "Truth Shall Set You Free," and if that doesn't work go talk to your sponsor. If you don't have one, well that is what this book is all about. I hope you enjoy it. I truly enjoyed writing and putting it together.

SantaC

Take your time working the 12 Steps...
What makes you think you've got time...???

My Big Book says. ..."we launched out on a course of vigorous action"

Taking the Steps

Steps... that sounds like some kind of movement...*Action*

IN THE BEGINNING

The book Alcoholics Anonymous, The Big Book as it is so fondly called, was written by and for the alcoholic that was diagnosed as a chronic, hopeless and an incurable drunk. They are still here today (2012 when this was written). You can find them in the missions, the Salvation Army, Volunteers of America, VOA and in the heart of any city but that is not what the majority of A.A. or any other 12 step program is made up of today.

We are going to stick to the basic principles that were set up over seventy plus years ago. What they did then and what you have to do now to be successful, a recovered person. These steps will work in any of the 12 step programs, if they are followed and practiced daily. As it says in the Big Book pg. XIII, "To show other alcoholics **precisely** how we **recovered** is the main purpose of this book."

THE TENT IS TO SMALL FOR THE CIRCUS

When I was a kid growing up the circus would come to town and set up at the Fairgrounds or in some farmer's large field. There would be a midway where you could play games of chance and maybe win a Teddy Bear and occasionally you would see someone walking around with one of the prized Bears but usually you threw your money away. Then there were the rides, bumper cars, Ferris Wheels, rides that would spin so fast that they would make you dizzy or sick. But the most exciting part of the Fair was the Big Top. Two to three times a day there was a show that you could go see. Usually there were three rings and you wanted to be sitting as close to the center ring as possible because that is where the best shows were going to be presented. In addition, that is where the clowns did all of their shenanigans and if you were lucky they might call on you to help them pull one off. Everything was well organized and choreographed to perfection.

After many failures, trials and errors, the founders of alcoholics anonymous had developed a system that if followed would expel the obsession to drink and let the individual live a productive life. They then documented that in a book called; Alcoholics Anonymous. They could tell an alcoholic *precisely* how to be a **Recovered** Alcoholic.

In the early years of our Fellowship a group of prominent psychiatrists studied our membership to determine what, if any, characteristics we alcoholics shared in common. The answer shocked the membership of that time. They said that we were CHILDISH, GRANDIOSE AND OVERLY SENSITIVE. Judging by the way the people act in A.A. today, we haven't changed much in the last 57 years (the time that passed when this was written). There is finger pointing, gossip, back stabbing, chair warmers, bleeding deacons, elder statesmen and the newcomer who ask themselves; "Do I really want what they have?" When a new person walks into the rooms of A.A., they are not sure what A.A. has to offer. Most of them are not even sure what they have much less what A.A. has. Then they get to hear individuals who are foul mouthed and in the same breath talk about spiritual principals.

There was this young lady who confronted me one day in my early sobriety and asked me if "I ate with the same mouth I spoke with?" As a direct result of her confrontation

I began to clean up my language. I for one am truly ashamed by the above behaviors and I hope that I am not the only one.

Our first tradition tells us that our personal recovery depends on A.A. unity and it is about time we started figuring out that we need to leave our oversized egos at the door when we come together as a body. Just because I'm an alcoholic, doesn't mean I can make excuses to continue to act like I just crawled out of a sewer pipe. I was told to grow up and start being responsible and accountable for my behavior.

There is no room for an ill-mannered membership that doesn't know how to act in public. There is no room for the divisiveness that has plagued A.A. for many years. The fellowship really needs to conduct an inventory on ourselves to insure we move into the future with the same love for A.A. that was demonstrated by our founding members.

It is every member's responsibility to insure our Fellowship survives the challenges presented to us in a respectable manner and act like the grown-ups we are intended to be. It is a Sponsors responsibility to point this out and show the new person what appropriate behavior is and what isn't. Let's focus on the center ring where the main show is and that is to carry the message to the still suffering alcoholic. To focus on the solution and the side shows in the smaller rings will fall into place.

MANY ROADS TO HELL ARE PAVED WITH GOOD INTENTIONS

Good intentions and 50 cents won't get you a cup of coffee today. After being around A.A. for a while my life was still a mess. I was the famous "Bull in the China Shop." You have heard that that saying; "Nothing changes unless something changes." I kept trying to work the Steps by myself. Guess what? As smart as I thought I was, I couldn't figure them out. I needed someone to help me take them. I had to learn that asking for help is not a sign of weakness but a sign of strength. If I have heard it once I've heard it a thousand times. I did them the best that I could. I don't believe I have "ever done the best I could," because I have never been put to the test of having to do my best! And as of this writing I am 35 years sober and 67 years old. As my Dad would so confidently say to me; "The Blind cannot lead the Blind," and after 35 years of observation and several years of looking at A.A.'s history we, A.A., are heading in the wrong direction. The tail is wagging the Dog. The newcomer is running A.A. into the history books of Failure, just as the Oxford Group and the Washingtonians lost their focus. And the Old-timers are just sitting by and letting it happen.

Through the efforts of Marty M., one of our earliest female members and the founder of the National Council on Alcoholism and Drug Dependence began to take shape in 1944. The Focus was to raise the awareness of the disease of Alcoholism and to lessen the Stigma of being Alcoholic. Her efforts were followed by others who felt that Alcoholism should be decriminalized and in the 70's that happened. There were treatment centers cropping up all over America because of the Hugh's Act (1976). A.A. was getting new members at an overwhelming rate. The meetings began to change along with how sponsorship was done. It wasn't very long and we had people sponsoring newcomers that had never taken the steps. They were and are called "Two

Steppers." Yes, they admitted they were Alcoholic and then they were trying to carry the message without having done the other ten steps that are after the 1st step and preceding the 12th step.

Then we have those who are not real alcoholics who have worked some of the steps, but not all of them, attempting to help a real alcoholic. Telling them that I didn't have to do that step or you don't need to do this or that and so the alcoholic doesn't get to have a spiritual awakening or spiritual conversion. Then you hear someone say, "He or She must not have wanted it," when that new person goes out and fails.

Instead of crawling into A.A. we now get medications' to detox us at the treatment centers; we wouldn't want anyone to feel some pain. No more "real" 12 step calls, we just pick them up and drop them off at the front door. And 28 days later they come walking back into A.A. with all of the answers. Except two: how to work the steps and stay sober.

We, A.A., have become a self-help program instead of a God help program. You will hear it is the meetings that will keep you sober…90 meetings in 90 days? A place to get your court cards signed. A.A. is a baby sitter for an hour to an hour and a half. There are big meeting halls, Alano Clubs and Fellowship halls. A.A. has become a big business. A buck is not enough; we must break the $1.00 donation. There is little to no talk about God or Jesus Christ. If you do bring up God and especially Jesus, someone will tell you, you are breaking traditions or we don't talk about Him here. You must read only "conference approved" literature. For an organization that has no rules, A.A. as a whole sure has a bunch of them (RULES).

If we don't return to the basics that the Founding members taught and used, A.A. will not be here for the newcomer. I cannot stay sober unless I develop a relationship with God, practice prayer and meditation, asking for His will and direction in my life and the power to carry that out. Plus carry the message to the newcomer. My job as a Sponsor is teaching, them, the newcomer, how to develop a lasting relationship with God, take the steps and to carry the same message they learned to another newcomer. It is kind of like Amway, you are taught how it works and you pass on what you what you were taught to your down line. You get five and then they get five, so on and so on. If it is not broke, don't fix it, and if it is broke, fix it. A.A. is Broke so let's fix it.

THE TRADITIONS IN A NUTSHELL

1. Unity- Hang together or die alone.
2. One Authority--- Higher power/God.
3. Inclusiveness of membership - only one requirement for membership.
4. Group independence – unless it affects A.A. as a whole.
5. Singleness of Purpose- Carry this message.
6. No Affiliation - No ties to any other entity.
7. Self-Supporting- we carry our own.
8. No Professional Class--- No paid sponsors/counselors.
9. Least possible organization - no ruling class.
10. Nonpartisanship - Our Fellowship is our only concern.
11. No one member is more important than the whole.
12. Spiritual Anonymity - do good deeds and don't get caught.

THE 12 STEPS IN PLAIN ENGLISH

1. Alcohol will kill me.
2. There's a power that wants me to live.
3. Do I want to live or die? (If you want to die, stop here).
4. Write about how I got to where I am.
5. Tell another person all about me. (Let God listen).
6. Want to change.
7. Ask a God to help me change.
8. Write down who I've hurt.
9. Fix what I can without hurting anyone else.
10. Accept that I'm human and will screw up. Fix it immediately.
11. Ask a God to show me how to live.
12. Keep doing 10 thru 12 and passing on 1 thru 12.

(Author: Deb C. as modified by SantaC.)

UNITY

According to the 12 and 12 "The unity of Alcoholics Anonymous is the most cherished quality our Society has." Think about it, we have an irresistible strength of purpose and action. Lives are recreated (sometimes created), families are reunited and employers reclaim valuable talent. All these things are accomplished through the application of the spiritual principles embodied in A.A.'s traditions and recovery program. We need each other to recover. Most of us have tried to stop on our own and at some point have failed. Yet we come to A.A. and the most hopeless find recovery and acceptance in our groups. I've heard it said that you cannot recover without a group. That is not entirely true, our early founders didn't have groups, they carried the message to individuals one and two at a time and eventually small groups were formed. But it is NOT necessary to have a group; my book tells me I can carry the message anywhere. All I have to do is contact some doctors, jails, institutions, hospitals, religious people and eventually I will find someone who will want the message of recovery. But it is best to work in pairs.

"When, therefore, we A.A.s look to the future, we must always ask ourselves if the spirit which now binds us together in our common cause will always be stronger than those personal ambitions and desires which tend to drive us apart. Though the individual A.A. is under no human coercion, is at almost perfect personal liberty, we have, nevertheless, achieved a wonderful unity on vital essentials." (Bill W.)

DISCUSSION TOPIC: BACK TO BASICS
(April, 1976)

Are we, in the content of our A.A. meetings, getting away from basics?

Are we talking about our own recovery from alcoholism?

The Big Book, Twelve Steps and Twelve Traditions ?
(Bob B, Delegate, Northeast Ohio)

(Excerpts from his talk)
My name is Bob B. I am powerless over alcohol and very grateful to be alive. Are we, in the content of our A.A. meetings, getting away from A.A. basics? I believe we are. Alcoholics Anonymous is growing at a faster rate than at any time since the '40's, and I suspect we were not ready for such growth. Have we gotten a little complacent and smug in our well-being? People today are coming to Alcoholics Anonymous in far better shape physically and mentally than most of us here did. We need to show them how we learned to stay sober. If our meetings consist mostly of drinking experiences, our ideas and opinions, we are not doing our jobs. Dr. Bob said our program when boiled down, is love

and service (by service he means carrying the message, the solution, of recovery to the newcomer).

We need to show all the newcomers that we love them as we were loved and we have a way of life we wish to share. If our meetings are nothing but drunk-a-logs and meaningless chatter, we are not showing them "How It Works". In A.A. meetings, we reach out with love and tell people, "These are the Steps we took" and "We had to go to any lengths." Is that what the newcomer is hearing in our meetings today? (It is A.A.'s responsibility to carry the solution to the newcomer. It is not the new person's responsibility to ask for the message).

When a person comes to us after 30 days in a rehabilitation center, he or she is already dry and needs to know how we are staying sober. I believe our meetings are not really covering this heavy responsibility as effectively as we should and could. We do have some good news, such as Big Book Study Meetings. More and more in my area, we are going to discussion meetings. This new idea is from the Grapevine.

To me, it is vital to the survival of our Fellowship that we make certain the people coming to us for help are made aware of the Big Book, the Twelve Steps and Twelve Traditions as possibly their only hope for survival from alcoholism. If we fail to guide them to our program of recovery, our Fellowship will not survive. Our future (and the message) is dependent upon a continuing stream of recovered alcoholics.

In today's frustrating world, our Program works better than ever. Are we doing a good enough job sharing this with the thousands of people coming to us now? Shouldn't we be giving these people all Three Legacies of Recovery, Unity and Service? We have to tell them more than, "Don't drink and go to meetings". If all we talk about is our drinking, our ideas, our opinions, my day or the way I do it, we are not carrying the message--we are carrying the illness. We should be talking about recovery. I don't believe we are.

Are we stressing the real value of the Big Book? You can go to meetings in my area where you can't find a Big Book. Lately, when I am asked to lead a meeting, I have to take my Big Book with me. I don't want to lead a meeting that doesn't have a Big Book. We hear many people lead meetings and never mention the Steps or the Big Book. Is it because nobody told them how very important the Big Book is? Do we forget to tell the newcomer that what is in the Big Book can save his or her life? Our total Program is in the Big Book and only in the Big Book. Shouldn't we be telling people that?

We hear a lot of ridiculous things like, "There are no musts in A.A." My Big Book reads different. People say that it is an individual program that we can take the Steps any way we want to. Dr. Bob said, and I quote, "There is no such thing as an individual interpretation of the Twelve Steps." If we are not honest with the new people and tell them how important each Step is who will tell them? Some people seem to think the Steps are a necessary evil instead of a lifesaving prescription for happiness.

We rarely hear about the Traditions. The fact that these came about because of our Mistakes and failures is almost a secret. The Traditions are the lifesaving guide Lines for each group and for our Fellowship as a whole and each of us should be responsible to honor them. When I first wanted to get a copy of the "Twelve and Twelve", a Tradition pamphlet had all I needed. Thanl listen to him.

In 1965 at Maple Leaf Gardens in Toronto, most of us stood with Bill and said, "I am responsible. When anyone, anywhere reaches out for help, I want the hand of A.A. always to be there and for that I am responsible." Being at that Convention is the reason I am standing here now. We are the guardians of this Fellowship, and maybe we need to do a better job of sharing what it is all doubt. Are we still responsible?

Most things can be preserved in alcohol.

Dignity, however, is not one of them.

GOD SHOTS

- God loves everyone, but probably prefers "fruits of the spirit" over "religious nuts!"
- God promises a safe landing, not a calm passage.
- He who angers you, controls you!
- If God is your Copilot – swap seats:
- Most people want to serve God, but only in an advisory capacity.
- Prayer: Don't give God instructions – just report for duty!.
- The task ahead of us is never as great as the Power behind us.
- The Will of God will never take you to where the Grace of God will not protect you.
- We don't change the message, the message changes us.
- You can tell how big a person is by what it takes to discourage them.

Dr. Bob did very little writing; he was mostly in the trenches helping people put their lives back together. But not so with Clarence S. one of Dr. Bob's early sponsees. When sobriety found Clarence he was on fire. His story can be found in the first, second and third editions of the Big Book titled the "Brewmeister" and his biography is on-line. The title is "How It Worked" by Mitchell K.

A.A. SPONSORSHIP PAMPHLET
by Clarence S. (1944)

This is the first pamphlet ever written concerning sponsorship. It was written by Clarence H. S. in early 1944. Its original title was to be "A.A. Sponsorship...Its Obligations and Its Responsibilities." It was printed by the Cleveland Central Committee under the title:

"A.A. Sponsorship... Its Opportunities and Its Responsibilities."

PREFACE

Each member of Alcoholics Anonymous is a potential sponsor of a new member and should clearly recognize the obligations and duties of such responsibility.

The acceptance of an opportunity to take the A.A. plan to a sufferer of alcoholism entails very real and critically important responsibilities. Each member, undertaking the sponsorship of a fellow alcoholic, must remember that he is offering what is frequently the last chance of rehabilitation, sanity or maybe life itself.

Happiness, Health, Security, Sanity and Life of human beings are the things we hold in balance when we sponsor an alcoholic.

No member among us is wise enough to develop a sponsorship program that can be successfully applied in every case. In the following pages, however, we have outlined a suggested procedure, which supplemented by the member's own experience, has proven successful.

PERSONAL GAINS OF BEING A SPONSOR

No one reaps full benefit from any fellowship he is connected with unless he whole-heartedly engages in its important activities. The expansion of Alcoholics Anonymous to wider fields of greater benefit to more people results directly from the addition of new, worth-while members or associates.

Any A.A. who has not experienced the joys and satisfaction of helping another alcoholic regain his place in life has not yet fully realized the complete benefits of this fellowship. On the other hand, it must be clearly kept in mind that the only possible reason for bringing an alcoholic into A.A. is for that person's gain. Sponsorship should never be undertaken to –

1. Increase the size of the group.
2. For personal satisfaction and glory.
3. Because the sponsor feels it his duty to re-make the world.

Until an individual has assumed the responsibility of setting a shaking, helpless human being back on the path toward becoming a healthy useful, happy member of society, he has not enjoyed the complete thrill of being an A.A...

SOURCE OF NAMES

Most people have among their own friends and acquaintances someone who would benefit from our teachings. Others have names given to them by their church, by their doctor, by their employer, or by some other member, who cannot make a direct contact.

Because of the wide range of the A.A. activities, the names often come from unusual and unexpected places. These cases should be contacted as soon as all facts such as: marital status, domestic relations, financial status, drink habits, employment status and others readily obtainable are at hand.

IS THE PROSPECT A CANDIDATE?

Much time and effort can be saved by learning as soon as possible if -

1. The man* really has a drinking problem?

2. Does he know he has a problem?
3. Does he want to do something about his drinking?
4. Does he want help?

*The masculine form is used throughout for simplicity, although it is intended to include women as well.

Sometimes the answers to these questions cannot be made until the prospect has had some A.A. instruction, and an opportunity to think. Often we are given names, which upon investigation, show the prospect is in no sense an alcoholic, or are satisfied with his present plan of living. We should not hesitate to drop these names from our lists. Be sure, however, to let the man know where he can reach us at a later date.

WHO SHOULD BECOME MEMBERS?

A.A. is a fellowship of men and women bound together by their inability to use alcohol in any form sensibly, or with profit or pleasure. Obviously, any new members introduced should be the same kind of people, suffering from the same disease.

Most people can drink reasonably, but we are only interested in those who cannot. *Party drinkers, social drinkers, celebrators, and others who continue to have more pleasure than pain from their drinking, are of no interest to us.*

In some instances an individual might believe himself to be a social drinker when he definitely is an alcoholic. In many such cases more time must pass before that person is ready to accept our program. Rushing such a man before he is ready might ruin his chances of ever becoming a successful A.A... Do not ever deny future help by pushing too hard in the beginning.

Some people, although definitely alcoholic, have no desire or ambition to better their way of living, and until they do........ A.A. has nothing to offer them. ("Never deny anyone the Privilege of suffering." SantaC)

Experience has shown that age, intelligence, education, background, or the amount of liquor drunk, has little, if any, bearing on whether or not the person is an alcoholic.

PRESENTING THE PLAN

In many cases a man's physical condition is such that he should be placed in a hospital, if at all possible. Many A.A. members believe hospitalization, with ample time for the prospect to think and plan his future, free from domestic and business worries, offers distinct advantage. In many cases the hospitalization period marks the beginning of a new life. Other members are equally confident that any man who desires to learn the A.A. plan for living can do it in his own home or while engaged in normal occupation. Thousands of cases are treated in each manner and have proved satisfactory.

SUGGESTED STEPS*

The following paragraphs outline a suggested procedure for presenting the A.A. plan to the prospect, at home or in the hospital.

QUALIFY AS AN ALCOHOLIC

1. In calling upon a new prospect, it has been found best to qualify oneself as an ordinary person who has found

happiness, contentment, and peace of mind through A.A...
Immediately make it clear to the prospect that you are a
person engaged in the routine business of earning a living.
Tell him your only reason for believing yourself able to help
him is because you yourself are an alcoholic and have had
experiences and problems that might be similar to his.

TELL YOUR STORY*

2. Many members have found it desirable to launch
immediately into their personal drinking story, as a means of
getting the confidence and whole-hearted co-operation of the
prospect.

It is important in telling the story of your drinking life to tell
it in a manner that will describe an alcoholic, rather than a
series of humorous drunken parties. This will enable the
man to get a clear picture of an alcoholic which should help
him to more definitely decide whether he is an alcoholic.

INSPIRE CONFIDENCE IN A.A.*

3. In many instances the prospect will have tried various
means of controlling his drinking, including hobbies,

church, changes of residence, change of associations, and various control plans. These will, of course, have been unsuccessful. Point out your series of unsuccessful efforts to control drinking...their absolute fruitless results and yet that you were able to stop drinking through application of A.A. principles. This will encourage the prospect to look forward with confidence to sobriety in A.A. in spite of the many past failures he might have had with other plans.

4. Tell the prospect frankly that he cannot quickly understand all the benefits that are coming to him through A.A. Tell him of the happiness, peace of mind, health, and in many cases, material benefits which are possible through understanding and application of the A.A. way of life.

SHOW IMPORTANCE OF READING BOOK*

5. Explain the necessity of studying and re-reading the A.A. book. Point out that this book gives a detailed description of the A.A. tools and the suggested methods of application of these tools to build a foundation of rehabilitation for living. This is a good time to emphasize the importance of the

twelve steps and the four absolutes. ("Honesty, Unselfishness, Love and Purity.")

QUALITIES REQUIRED FOR SUCCESS IN A.A.*

6. Convey to the prospect that the objectives of A.A. are to provide the ways and means for an alcoholic to regain his normal place in life. Desire, patience, faith, study and application are most important in determining each individual's plan of action in gaining full benefits of A.A...
INTRODUCE FAITH*

7. Since the belief of a Power greater than oneself is the heart of the A.A. plan, and since this idea is very often difficult for a new man, the sponsor should attempt to introduce the beginnings of an understanding of this all-important feature.

Frequently this can be done by the sponsor relating his own difficulty in grasping a spiritual understanding and the methods he used to overcome his difficulties.

LISTEN TO HIS STORY*

8. While talking to the newcomer, take time to listen and study his reactions in order that you can present your information in a more effective manner. Let him talk too. Remember...Easy Does It.

TAKE TO SEVERAL MEETINGS*

9. To give the new member a broad and complete picture of A.A., the sponsor should take him to various meetings within convenient distance of his home. Attending several meetings gives a new man a chance to select a group in which he will be most happy and comfortable, and it is extremely important to let the prospect make his own decision as to which group he will join. Impress upon him that he is always welcome at any meeting and can change his home group if he so wishes.

EXPLAIN A.A. TO PROSPECT'S FAMILY*

10. A successful sponsor takes pains and makes any required effort to make certain that those people closest and with the greatest interest in their prospect (mother, father, wife, etc.) are fully informed of A.A., its principles and its objectives.

The sponsor sees that these people are invited to meetings, and keeps them in touch with the current situation regarding the prospect at all times.

HELP PROSPECT ANTICIPATE THE HOSPITAL EXPERIENCE*

11. A prospect will gain more benefit from a hospitalization period if the sponsor describes the experience and helps him anticipate it, paving the way for those members who will call on him.

CONSULT OLDER MEMBERS IN A.A.*

These suggestions for sponsoring a new man in A.A. teachings are by no means complete. They are intended only for a framework and general guide. Each individual case is different and should be treated as such. Additional information for sponsoring a new man can be obtained from the experience of older men in the work. A co-sponsor, with an experienced and newer member working on a prospect, has proven very satisfactory. Before undertaking the responsibility of sponsoring, a member should make certain that he is able and prepared to give the time, effort, and thought such an obligation entails. It might be that he will want to select a co-sponsor to share the responsibility, or he might feel it necessary to ask another to assume the responsibility for the man he has located.

WHEN YOU BECOME A SPONSOR...
BE A GOOD ONE!

WAYS TO STOP DRINKING

There are two types of serious drinkers; drunks and alcoholics. The drunk is one who usually drinks as a means to escape and can stop drinking or drink moderately if given a good reason to do so. On the other hand, <u>the alcoholic is one who cannot stop drinking by their own will-power no matter how great the necessity or the wish</u>. As an old saying goes, "<u>A drunk could quit if they would. An alcoholic would quit if they could.</u>" There is a significant difference.

<u>Ways to Stop Drinking</u>

<u>Covered Up</u>	<u>Locked up</u>	<u>Sobered Up</u>
Death	Jail, Prison or Mental Institution	A vital Spiritual Spiritual Experience
(This will do it)	(For a period of time)	(as long as we apply the Spiritual Principles)

It would appear that a vital Spiritual Experience would be the best choice of the three known ways to "stop drinking". <u>Unfortunately, most alcoholics will stop drinking only as the result of death</u>.

The distinguished American psychologist, William James, in his book, "Varieties of Religious Experience," indicates a multitude of ways in which men have discovered God. Down through the ages, there have been numerous reports of people experiencing a life changing conversion or personality change in the way they think and the way they feel sufficient to bring about a Solution to their life threatening problem. The Salvation Army, with its Christian Program, has been helping alcoholics find a way to a sober life since 1865. But probably the most effective, simple, clear-cut, time-tested and experience proven way to find the spiritual solution is through the Twelve Steps of Alcoholics Anonymous. This Program has proved to be very successful for *those alcoholics who have been willing to go to any length for victory over alcohol* and is clearly described in the Basic Text for Alcoholics Anonymous, "ALCOHOLICS ANONYMOUS" the "Big Book" as it is called in the Fellowship of Alcoholics Anonymous.

For those who really want to find a way out, the First Step is to understand the Problem - Alcoholism. There can be no solution till the problem is identified. "We admitted we were powerless over alcohol -- that our lives had become unmanageable". This Step contains two separate thoughts. In the "DOCTOR'S OPINION", we learn that the alcoholic is "powerless" over alcohol because of an allergy to alcohol that manifests itself as a "craving" for more alcohol once the alcoholic commences to drink. So once the alcoholic starts drinking, they invariably drink too much although it seems to them that they can never get enough. Often, this excessive drinking leads to problems that cause the alcoholic to make a decision that they have had enough. They are going to quit forever. Unfortunately, most real alcoholics are beyond the point where they can say "I quit and stay that way. In a short period of time, (hours, days, weeks or at the most a few months) they find themselves back at the game and they cannot tell you why. Even when they have been told they are going to lose the job, or their wife is leaving them for good this time or they are going back to jail because it is a parole violation they will find themselves taking another drink and they are off to the races again. In spite of the repeated misery, degradation, humiliation and loss of so many things of real value, they cannot stay away from the first drink They lack the power, that will power or self-will that is so necessary to resist the need for that drink. [So that you know what I am talking about, my friend was only going to have a couple drinks and two months later he shows up at his home. The wife has changed all of the locks and had moved all of his belongings into the garage. So much for controlled drinking it just doesn't work for the real alcoholic.]

Medical Science has found that there is sound reasoning in the "Doctor's Opinion". <u>Our DNA is different from the non-alcoholic.</u>

A Gene for Alcoholism is Discovered

Researchers at Washington University and 5 other centers have combined forces to identify a gene that is associated with alcoholism in some families. The scientists focused on a region of chromosome 15 that contains several genes involved in the movement of a brain chemical called GABA between neurons. One version of the gene, GABRG3, was found statistically linked (associated) with alcoholism in the affected families. (www.medicinenet.com)

If a person is not an alcoholic they can drink all they want. They can get DUI's, in trouble with the law, their wives or employers. They can become a hard drinker and show all the signs of alcoholism but given sufficient reason they can quit. No matter what they do or what anyone says; they cannot become an alcoholic because they don't have the genes to become one..

> "Quite as important was the fact that spiritual principles would solve ***all my problems***. I have since been brought into a way of living infinitely more satisfying and, I hope, more useful that the life I lived before. My old manner of life was by no means a bad one, but I would not exchange the best moments for the worst I have now. I would not go back to it even if I could."   (Big Book, Page 42 - 43)

[Look at the numbers then (75% to 93% in the Ohio area) and the numbers today! (Less than 5% nationwide) I can go to a meeting in my area where there are regularly 125 people every Wednesday night. Within a (4) four month period there is usually an 85% to 90% turnover. My question is: "If these people are looking for sobriety? Why aren't they getting it?"]

That question is being asked by a lot of alcoholics lately. What happened to our high success rate? 30 & 40 years ago, we were keeping 75% or more of the alcoholics who came to us for help. Today, we aren't keeping even 5%. What happened?

[A.A. might take a look at the success of long ago. They didn't have big meetings or meeting halls, Alano Clubs or Fellowship buildings. The early members held their meetings across the kitchen table. Once a week they would all meet at one of the homes to discuss how to help the newcomer. Their families were included in the recovery process. Everybody helped and shared their recourses amongst themselves.]

Bill W. wrote,
"In the years ahead A.A. will, of course, make mistakes. Experience has taught us that we need have no fear of doing this, **providing that we always remain willing to admit our faults and to correct them promptly**. Our growth as individuals has depended upon this healthy process of trial and error. So will our growth as a fellowship.

Let us always remember that any society of men and women that cannot freely correct its own faults must surely fall into decay if not into collapse. Such is the universal penalty for the failure to go on growing. Just as each A.A. must continue to take his moral inventory and act upon it, so must our whole Society if we are to survive and if we are to serve usefully and well." (A.A. Comes of Age, pg. 231)

With so very few finding lasting sobriety and the continued demise of A.A. groups, it is obvious that we have not **remained willing to admit our faults and to correct them promptly.**

So it seems to me that the Delegate of the Northeast Ohio Area, Bob B, identified our mistakes and our faults when he talked to a group of A.A.'s in 1976. He said, in essence, we are no longer showing the newcomer that we have a solution for alcoholism. We are not telling them about the Big Book and how very important that Book, sponsorship and carrying then message is to our long term sobriety. We are not talking about the solution and showing the newcomer how to take the steps. And then to teach the newcomer how to pass on what was so freely given to them. That is why A.A. is dying. The new people are not learning How It Works and the Old Timers who know how it works are dying off or they are getting a little depressed and taking a few pills so they can sleep or feel better and the next thing you know, they have broke out drunk and are newcomers again if they didn't die.

If you go to the Library of Congress and look for the book, Alcoholics Anonymous, you will find it in the Self Help section. We are not a Self Help Program; *We are a God Help Program.*

You can't have a solution if you don't know what the problem is or you don't believe you have a problem. Go to five different meetings and you will be hard pressed to hear the solution discussed. Oh, you will hear about a lot of problems, and yes everyone has problems but I came here to save my life and help save the lives of others. Bill W. stayed sober because he was willing to help someone else find sobriety through a Spiritual Experience. To develop a relationship with God and to follow God's will in his everyday living. Let's get back on track carrying the message of recovery as it was carried 70 years ago.

I have heard people told not to make any major decisions in their first year of sobriety. Isn't quitting drinking a major decision? How about turning your life over to the care of God, isn't that a major decision? How about carrying the message of recovery and becoming responsible and accountable for my actions, isn't that a major decision?

A sponsor's job is to get the new person hooked up with God as quickly as possible and *Un-hooked from the sponsor "As Soon As Possible."* I see people with years of not drinking; asking their sponsor what should they do? Something is wrong in that kind of relationship. I should be seeking God's will in my life, NOT my sponsors!

With the advent of treatment centers and detox hospitals A.A. lost its advantage of working with the wet newcomer. By the time they get to A.A. they had a head full of information about alcoholism, but no idea on how to be recovered. Besides they are feeling pretty good and are beginning to question, *well maybe I'm not that bad.* Maybe I can handle this by myself. The insurance company paid for it, so there was no money out of their pocket.

What do these guys have to teach me, I just finished 4 weeks of intensive therapy?

When they first went in to the treatment environment they were teachable, four to six weeks later, they know everything. Those who know how to work the steps and try to show them the solution run into a brick wall. In a very short time the new person is drunk and wonders why. A.A. doesn't work and neither does going to a treatment center.

When A.A. was very successful, the folks who did the talking in meetings were recovered alcoholics. The suffering and untreated alcoholics listened. After hearing what it takes to recover, the newcomer was faced with a decision; "Are you going to take the Steps and recover or are you going to get back out there and finish the job?" If they were willing to go to any length, they were assigned a sponsor, given a Big Book and taken through the Steps. They were then qualified to pass the program on to another newcomer. This all happened in one or two weeks, usually less than a month. Our growth rate was approximately 7% and the number of sober members of Alcoholics Anonymous doubled every 10 years.

With the advent of the rapid growth of the Treatment Industry, the acceptance of our success with alcoholics by the judicial system and endorsement of physicians, psychiatrist, psychologist, etc. all kinds of people were pouring into A.A. at a rate greater than we had ever dreamed possible. Almost without realizing what was happening, our meetings began changing from ones that focused on the solution to alcoholism to "discussion or participation" meetings where anyone could talk about any subject that was bothering them. The meetings went from solution oriented to the group therapy or my wife she, my boss he meetings where we heard more about "our problems" and less and less about the solution and how to be a Recovered alcoholic.

What has been the result of all this? Never have so many come to A.A. looking for help and not getting the answer. Is everyone who is coming to A.A. a real alcoholic? No; but those who are real alcoholics looking for help are not getting it. For the first time in our history, Alcoholics Anonymous is losing members faster than they are coming in and our success rate is unbelievably low. (Statistics from the Inter-Group Office of some major cities indicate less than 5% of those expressing a desire to stop drinking are successful for more than 5 years; a far cry from the 75% reported by Bill W. in the Forward to Second Edition) (Dr. Bob's sponsee, Clarence S., brought the Akron program to Cleveland and achieved a documented, 93% success rate in Cleveland as reported by Dick B. - www.dickb.com). The change in the content of our meetings is proving to be death-traps for the newcomer and in turn, ultimately failure for A.A. as a whole.

Treatment centers encouraged their clients to "just go to meetings and don't drink" or worse yet, "go to 90 meetings in 90 days". The newcomer is no longer told to take the Steps or get back out there and finish the job. In fact, they are often told, "Don't rush into taking the Steps. Take your time." The alcoholics who participated in the writing of the Big Book didn't wait. They took the Steps in the first few days or weeks following their last drink.

Thank God, there are those in our Fellowship, like Joe & Charlie, Wally P., Whiskey Bill etc., who have recognized the problem and have started doing something about it. They are placing the focus back on the Big Book where the directions are. There are individuals that carry the message of recovery to the suffering alcoholic. That is to tell the newcomer that "we have had a spiritual awakening as the result of these Steps and if you want to recover, we will see that you have a sponsor who has recovered and will lead you along the path the 1st 100 laid down for us". Recovered alcoholics have begun taking the newcomer through the Big Book and taking them through the steps. The newcomer is informed that until they have taken the steps and recovered, they will not be permitted to say anything in meetings. They will listen to recovered alcoholics, they will take the Steps, they will recover and then they will try to pass their experience and knowledge on to the ones who are seeking the kind of help we provide in Alcoholics Anonymous. As this movement spreads, as it is beginning to, Alcoholics Anonymous will again be very successful in doing the one thing God intended for us to do and that is to help the suffering alcoholic recover, if he has decided he wants what we have and is willing to go to any length to get it: "To be a recovered alcoholic."

There is a tendency to want to place the blame for our predicament on the treatment industry and other professionals. The real problem is that the members of Alcoholics Anonymous have gotten lazy. They have let the tail wag the dog, so to speak. It is time to bring the program back to the kitchen table. It is time to leave the big meetings and if not leave them, at least be a voice with the solution or perhaps change the meeting formats. Eliminate or change the discussion meeting formats to meetings run by recovered alcoholics.

When I am working with a new person, they cannot share during meetings. If called upon they can state their name, say they are alcoholic, they are working the steps and have a sponsor. Until they have finished working the first nine steps that is what they share. Before and after the meeting they can talk up a storm about anything, including what they know about the solution or they can talk about me.

So there we are. We have had 30 years of unbelievable success by following the directions of the early founders. Now we have 35 years of disappointing failure by wanting to hear from everyone.

Now we have something to compare.

We now know what the problem is and we know what the solution is. Unfortunately, we have not been prompt in correcting our faults and mistakes which have been created by what would appear to be large doses of indifference and complacency. The problems we are living with is pointlessly killing alcoholics. What is the Solution? Let's get back to the basics in the Big Book and the Bible, Dr. Bob's source for solutions and the guidelines established by some of our founding members.

WHAT IS A SPONSOR?

SPONSOR - "One who assumes, or one to whom is delegated, responsibility for some other person." or - "One who at the baptism of an infant professes the Christian faith in its name, and guarantees its religious {spiritual} education." ("We were reborn." A.A., pg. 63)
Webster, circa - 1936

Step Twelve reads, *"Having had a spiritual awakening as the result of these steps, we tried to carry this message to alcoholics, and to practice these principles in all our affairs."*

That, of course, is what a Sponsor is. He is an alcoholic who has taken these Steps and had a spiritual awakening or spiritual experience or an entire psychic change. That is described on pages 83 and 84 in our Basic Text, Alcoholics Anonymous.

Let's see what that Book has to say about a Sponsor (a recovered alcoholic):

"But the ex-problem drinker who has found this solution, who is properly armed with facts about himself, can generally wins the confidence of another alcoholic in a few hours. Until such an understanding is reached, little or nothing can be accomplished." (A.A., Pg. 18)

How does he do that? Well, <u>the effective sponsor has studied Chapter Seven, "Working With Others"</u>.

1. His first job then is to see if the prospect appears to be willing to go to any length to achieve victory over alcohol, (A.A., pg. 90).

2. His second job is to see if he has a <u>REAL ALCOHOLIC</u> to work with, (A.A., pg. 92). If he is not, try to help them find the fellowship that deals with their problem.
    (A.A. page 44, para.1 describes the alcoholic)

3. His third job is to give the prospect a killer case of alcoholism so he will feel totally hopeless and helpless, (A.A., pg. 92).

4. Then, his fourth job is to give the prospect hope, (A.A., pg. 93).

5. His fifth job is to see if the prospect is, in fact, willing to go to any length (A.A., pg. 94 - 96) to achieve victory over alcohol. (That is to see they have a copy of the Big Book and are willing to carefully read it to determine if they are willing to adopt the Program as a way of life)

6. If he is, then his sixth job is to start the protégé on his journey to sobriety by taking Steps Three, Four and Five, (A.A., pg. 96).

7. His seventh job is to walk with his protégé in putting the remaining Steps to work until he is solid in living our Program, one day at a time (A.A., pg. 96 - 103).

8. Once the protégé has found a newcomer and has effectively passed this on to another suffering alcoholic, you will have done your job and know joy of living, which is giving that others may live. (A.A., pg. 163 – 164)

9.	Continue to look for the next prospect.

Is Sponsorship important? Let's see what the Big Book reports.

"For if an alcoholic failed to perfect and enlarge his spiritual life through work and self-sacrifice for others, he could not survive the certain trials and low spots ahead" (A.A., pg. 14 & 15).

"Our very lives, as ex-problem drinkers, depend upon our constant thought of others and how we may help meet their needs."   (A.A., pg. 20)

"Practical experience shows nothing will so much insure immunity from drinking as intensive work with other alcoholics. It works when other activities fail." (A.A., pg. 89)

AND AS DR. BOB REPORTED:

"I spend a great deal of time passing on what I learned to others who want and need it badly. I do it for four reasons:

1. Sense of duty.
2. It is a pleasure.
3. Because in doing so I am paying my debt to the man who took time to pass it on to me.
4. Because every time I do it I take out a little more insurance for myself against a possible slip." (A.A., pg. 180 - 181)

Dr. Bob did take the matter of Sponsorship very seriously. History shows that he helped approximately 5,000 alcoholics experience the Promises of the Program of Alcoholics Anonymous over a 10 year period. That turns out to average 1.5 new alcoholics every day over that 10 year period. That would certainly qualify as "intensive" work with other alcoholics. That number is probably higher but in Dr. Bob's final years he was very sick with cancer.

So, it would appear to make sense, if we have been restored

to sanity where alcohol is concerned, to follow the directions the 1st 100 laid down for us in our Basic Text, "ALCOHOLICS ANONYMOUS" and apply the Twelfth Step Prayer as directed, which is: "Ask Him in you morning meditation what you can do *each day* for the man who is still sick. The answers will come, IF your own house is in order. But you obviously cannot transmit something you haven't got. See to it that your relationship with Him is right and great events will come to pass for you and countless others. This is the Great Fact for us." (A.A., pg. 164).

The Program of Alcoholics Anonymous works if we work it! We die if we don't!! So WORK it!!! (But that is only a suggestion)

ATTENTION!
ARE YOU:
Tired of being told like it is?
Still looking for that easier softer way?
Had enough of that same, old time-tested direction?
Then You Are Ready For:

RENT-A-SPONSOR

NO READING! NO WRITING! NO DEADLINES!
MANY MODELS FROM WHICH TO CHOOSE!

STANDARD FEATURES INCLUDE:
Listening to your sniveling without constant reference to the steps.
Co-signing your excuses and rationalizations.
Working with only the steps you want and in the order you choose **at**

RENT-A-SPONOR

We know how unique you are, and we do understand!
Learn the secret of giving it away before you even have it.
Why walk the walk when you can just talk the talk?
Remember it's better to look good than to feel good!
Why save your rear at the cost of losing face? •
Half measures are our specialty!

Call 1-900-POUR-ME-1

**CALL NOW AND RECEIVE A FREE COPY OF:
STAYING SOBER ON WAR STORIES ALONE**

WHAT EARLY A.A. WAS REALLY LIKE
by Dick B. (website)

"Alcoholics Anonymous, Alcoholics Anonymous History, Bill W., and Dr. Bob. This A.A. history website focuses particularly on the roles God, Jesus Christ, and the Bible had in early A.A.'s astonishing, documented, 75% and 93% success rates (in Akron and Cleveland, respectively) among "seemingly-hopeless," "medically-incurable," alcoholics who really tried to establish or re-establish their relationship with the God of the Bible through His Son Jesus Christ.

A.A. Cofounder Bill W.'s Helpful Quotes

"I'll do anything, anything at all. If there be a Great Physician, I'll call on him." [Bill W., *My First 40 Years: An Autobiography by the Cofounder of Alcoholics Anonymous* (Center City, Minn.: Hazelden, 2000), 145.]

"For sure I'd been born again."
[Bill W., *My First 40 Years*, 147.]

"Henrietta, the Lord has been so wonderful to me [Bill W.], curing me of this terrible disease, that I just want to keep talking about it and telling people." [*Alcoholics Anonymous*, 4th ed., Pg. 191.]

"I [Abby G.] wanted to know what this was that worked so many wonders, and hanging over the mantel was a picture of Gethsemane and Bill [W.] pointed to it and said, 'There it is,' ..." [*Alcoholics Anonymous*, 3rd ed. Pg. 216-17.]

The Success of Early A.A. as Reported in *Alcoholics Anonymous*

"Of alcoholics who came to A.A. and really tried, 50% got sober at once and remained that way; 25% sobered up after some relapses, and among the remainder, those who stayed on with A.A. showed improvement." [*Alcoholics Anonymous: The Story of How Many Thousands of Men and Women Have Recovered from Alcoholism*, 4th ed. Pg. XX]

The Alcoholics Anonymous Original "Program" as Was Reported by Frank Amos in *DR. BOB and the Good Oldtimers*

An alcoholic must realize that he is an alcoholic, incurable from a medical viewpoint, and that he must never drink anything with alcohol in it.

He must surrender himself absolutely to God, realizing that in himself there is no hope.

Not only must he want to stop drinking permanently, he must remove from his life other sins such as hatred, adultery, and others which frequently accompany alcoholism. Unless he will do this absolutely, Smith and his associates refuse to work with him.

He must have devotions every morning–a "quiet time" of prayer and some reading from the Bible and other religious literature. Unless this is faithfully followed, there is grave danger of backsliding.

He must be willing to help other alcoholics get straightened out. This throws up a protective barrier and strengthens his own willpower and convictions.

It is important, but not vital, that he meet frequently with other reformed alcoholics and form both a social and a religious comradeship.

Important, but not vital, that he attend some religious service at least once weekly. [*DR. BOB and the Good Oldtimers* (New York, N.Y.: Alcoholics Anonymous World Services, Inc., 1980), 131.]

Much of this information you won't find in A.A.'s basic text (*Alcoholics Anonymous*) today or in our Alcoholics Anonymous meetings. But the simplicity of the original, early Alcoholics Anonymous Society (A.A.) will really astound you! And we are here speaking about the pioneer A.A. Christian Fellowship in Akron that--at the hands of Bill W. and Dr. Bob--developed A.A.'s spiritual program of recovery and was led by Akron physician Dr. Bob by common consent. This Akron "Program"—with its five required elements and two optional ones--was thoroughly investigated, and reported on to John D. Rockefeller, Jr., by Rockefeller's agent, Frank Amos, who soon became one of A.A.'s first nonalcoholic trustees. [See *DR. BOB and the Good Oldtimers* (New York, N.Y.: Alcoholics Anonymous World Services, Inc., 1980), 128-36—especially 131.]

How It Worked

Abstinence was Number One. Usually there was hospitalization or at least medical help to save the newcomer's life. At the hospital, the only reading material allowed in the room was the Bible. Recovered Alcoholics Anonymous drunks visited the patient and told their success stories. Dr. Bob visited daily. And he would explain the "disease" or "illness," as it was then understood. The newcomer had to identify as an alcoholic, admit that he too was licked, and declare that he would do whatever it took to recover.

Reliance on the Creator was Number Two. *DR. BOB and the Good Oldtimers* records on page 144 the statement of Clarence S. (who brought A.A. to Cleveland) as to how A.A.

cofounder Dr. Bob talked with him about God while he (Clarence) was still in the hospital:

"Then he [Dr. Bob] asked, 'Do you believe in God, young fella?' (He always called me 'young fella.' When he called me Clarence, I knew I was in trouble.)

"What does that have to do with it?"

"Everything, he said."

"I guess I do."

"Guess, nothing! Either you do or you don't."

"Yes, I do."

"That's fine,' Dr. Bob replied. 'Now we're getting someplace. All right, get out of bed and on your knees.

We're going to pray."

"I don't know how to pray."

"I guess you don't, but that's all right. Just follow what I say, and that will do for now."

"I did what I was ordered to do," Clarence said. "There was no suggestion."

The Alcoholics Anonymous newcomer would very soon be given the opportunity to "surrender" upstairs in the home of an Akron A.A... This "surrender" involved the newcomer's confessing Jesus Christ as his personal Lord and Savior in a prayer session resembling what is described in James 5:14-16. (This confession of Christ by which the newcomer became born again has been confirmed as a "must" by four different and well-known A.A. old-timers—J. D. Holmes, Clarence Snyder, Larry Bauer, and Ed Andy.) At the time of the newcomer's "surrender," the "elders" (usually Dr. Bob, T. Henry Williams, and one other person) prayed with the newcomer that God would take alcohol out of his life, and joined him in asking God that He (God) would guide the newcomer so that he might live according to God's will.

Obedience to God's will was Number Three. Successful Alcoholics Anonymous members in Akron during the early years were expected to walk in love and to eliminate sinful conduct from their lives. Many newcomers were too sick to venture far from Akron; so they lived with the Smiths (and later others) in Akron homes. Early A.A. members who recovered from alcoholism with the help of Dr. Bob and other Akron A.A.s did not do so in an afternoon or in four easy lessons. They shook. They shivered. They fidgeted. They forgot. They were ashamed, insecure, and guilt-ridden. But they learned from the Good Book what a loving God had made available to them and that obedience to God's will was the key to receiving it.

Growth in Fellowship with their Heavenly Father was Number Four. At the homes in Akron, A.A.s had daily Quiet Time. This included Bible study, prayer, asking guidance from God, reading a devotional, and discussing selections from Anne Smith's journal. They shared their woes and problems with Dr. Bob, with Anne (his wife), and with Henrietta Seiberling. They also had personal Quiet Times at their homes and elsewhere when they were not together with other A.A.s. Alcoholics Anonymous members had one meeting a week. There were no "drunkalogs." There was no "whining." There was no "psychobabble."

They prayed, read from the Bible, and had Quiet Time. They used *The Upper Room* or similar devotionals for discussion.

Intensive help for other alcoholics was the Fifth element. Following the surrender of newcomers upstairs at the weekly meetings, announcements were made downstairs about Alcoholics Anonymous newcomers who had been placed at hospitals. Religious comradeship and attendance at a church of choice were the two recommended, but not required, elements of the Akron program. Socializing followed an A.A. meeting. And it started all over again. There were sessions with Dr. Bob involving doing a moral inventory (which related to adhering to the Four Absolutes—honest, purity, unselfishness, and love), confession, prayer to have the sins removed, and plans for restitution.

What Happened?

Did the Akron program work? You bet it did. Alcoholics Anonymous in Akron achieved a documented, 75% success rate among the "seemingly-hopeless," "medically-incurable" alcoholics who really tried. That success was primarily among Akron A.A. members. And the fact that they had been cured by the power of God was widely publicized across America. Soon, Dr. Bob's sponsee, Clarence S., brought the Akron program to Cleveland and achieved a documented, 93% success rate in Cleveland.

The same God (the Creator of the heavens and the earth), the same Lord and Savior Jesus Christ (the Son of the living God), and the same Bible (the Word of God) that helped early A.A.s in Akron and Cleveland recover from and be cured of alcoholism are still available today to help alcoholics and others suffering with "life-controlling" problems. The principles and practices of the early A.A. program in Akron and Cleveland were very similar to the basic principles that had also been working in the Salvation Army, the Rescue Missions, the YMCA, and Christian Endeavor. And they can and should be made available again today to those who still suffer.

And It Will Work Today!

Alcoholics Anonymous is certainly no longer a Christian fellowship (as it was in Akron); nor does it any longer require belief in God or even in anything at all. But, for those who do believe that the Creator of the heavens and the earth still can, and wants to, heal those suffering today, an accurate knowledge of A.A. history can help. That knowledge is vital too if the healing power of God is to be passed along to those in Alcoholics Anonymous who want it and who choose to receive it. As future A.A. nonalcoholic trustee Frank Amos reported to John D. Rockefeller, Jr., the early Akron A.A. program took abstinence, God, Jesus Christ, the Bible, a life-changing decision, living consistent with that decision, witnessing to others, fellowship with others, and time--lots of it. It was that simple. There were no "Steps," and there was no "textbook." The early A.A.s in Akron had Bibles. They had several Oxford Group precepts. They abstained from drinking and worked hard to avoid temptation. They relied on the Creator and His Son Jesus Christ. They endeavored to obey to God's will—both through eliminating sin and by living a life of love and service. They sought to grow in fellowship with the Father, with His Son Jesus Christ, and with each other through Bible study, prayer, asking God for wisdom, and studying devotionals and other Christian literature. That was the program that Bill W., Dr. Bob and his wife Anne, and the other early A.A. pioneers founded in Akron during the summer of 1935. And the principles of that program can still help, and are helping, those still suffering today. As Dr. Bob—whom A.A. cofounder Bill W. called "the prince of all twelfth steppers" because he had personally helped more than 5,000 alcoholics to recover—stated in the last line of his personal story on page 181 of the Fourth Edition of *Alcoholics Anonymous*:" Dick B. http://www.dickb.com/

A MANUAL FOR ALCOHOLICS ANONYMOUS

From A.A. Group No. 1, Akron, Ohio, 1940
Dr. Bob's Home Group

(Editor's Note, 1997: Dr. Bob probably wrote or heavily influenced the writing and distribution of this pamphlet. Dr. Bob was the Prince of 12 Steppers, from the day he achieved permanent sobriety, June 10, 1935, the founding date of Alcoholics Anonymous, until his death, November 16, 1950, carrying the message of A.A. to well over 5000 men and women alcoholics, and to all these he gave his medical services without thought of charge).

FOREWORD

This booklet is intended to be a practical guide for new members and sponsors of new members of Alcoholics Anonymous.

TO THE NEWCOMER: The booklet is designed to give you a practical explanation of what to do and what not to do in your search for sobriety. The editors, too, were pretty bewildered by the program at first. They realize that very likely you are groping for answers and offer this pamphlet in order that it may make a little straighter and less confusing the highway you are about to travel.

****

TO THE SPONSOR: If you have never before brought anyone into A.A. the booklet attempts to tell you what your duties are by your "Baby," how you should conduct yourself while visiting patients, and other odd bits of information, some of which may be new to you.

The booklet should be read in conjunction with the large book, Alcoholics Anonymous, the Bible, the daily lesson, any other pamphlets that are published by the group, and other constructive literature. A list of suggestions will be found in the back pages of this pamphlet. It is desirable that members of A.A. furnish their prospective "Babies" with this "Manual" as early as possible, particularly in the case of hospitalization.

The experience behind the writing and editing of this pamphlet adds up to hundreds of years of drinking, plus scores of years of recent sobriety. Every suggestion, every word, is backed up by hard experience.

The editors do not pretend any explanation of the spiritual or religious aspects of A.A. It is assumed that this phase of the work will be explained by sponsors. The booklet therefore deals solely with the physical aspects of getting sober and remaining sober.

A.A. in Akron is fortunate in having facilities for hospitalizing its patients. In many communities, however, hospitalization is not available. Although the pamphlet mentions hospitalization throughout, the methods described are effective if the patient is confined to his home, if he is in prison or a mental institution, or if he is attempting to learn A.A. principles and carry on his workaday job at the same time.

If your community has a hospital, either private or general, that has not accepted alcoholic patients in the past, it might be profitable to call on the officials of the institution and explain Alcoholics Anonymous to them. Explain that we are not in the business of sobering up drunks merely to have them go on another bender. Explain that our aim is total and permanent sobriety. Hospital authorities should know, and if they do not, should be told, that ==an alcoholic is a sick man, just as sick as a diabetic== or a consumptive. Perhaps his affliction will not bring death as quickly as diabetes or tuberculosis, but it will bring death or insanity eventually.

Alcoholism has had a vast amount of nationwide publicity in recent years. It has been discussed in medical journals, national magazines and newspapers. It is possible that a little sales talk will convince the hospital authorities in your community that they should make beds available for patients sponsored by Alcoholics Anonymous.

If the way is finally opened, it is urged that you guard your hospital privileges carefully. Be as certain as you possibly can be that your patient sincerely wants A.A.

Above all, carefully observe all hospital rules.

It has been our experience that a succession of unruly patients or unruly visitors can bring a speedy termination of hospital privileges. And they will want no part of you or your patient in the future.

Once he starts to sober up, the average alcoholic makes a model hospital patient. He needs little or no nursing or medical care, and he is grateful for his opportunity.

I - Definition of an Alcoholic Anonymous:

An Alcoholic Anonymous is an alcoholic who through application of and adherence to rules laid down by the organization, has completely forsworn the use of any and all alcoholic beverages. The moment he wittingly drinks so much as a drop of beer, wine, spirits, or any other alcoholic drink he automatically loses all status as a member of Alcoholics Anonymous.

A.A. is not interested in sobering up drunks who are not sincere in their desire to remain completely sober for all time. A.A. is not interested in alcoholics who want to sober up merely to go on another bender, sober up because of fear for their jobs, their wives, their social standing, or to clear up some trouble either real or imaginary. In other words, if a person is genuinely sincere in his desire for continued sobriety for his own good, is convinced in his heart that alcohol holds him in its power, and is willing to admit that he is an alcoholic, members of Alcoholics Anonymous will do all in their power, spend days of their time to guide him to a new, a happy, and a contented way of life.

It is utterly essential for the newcomer to say to himself, sincerely and without any reservation, "I am doing this for myself and myself alone." Experience has proved in hundreds of cases that unless an alcoholic is sobering up for a purely personal and selfish motive, he will not remain sober for any great length of time. He may remain sober for a few weeks or a few months, but the moment the motivating element, usually fear of some sort, disappears, so disappears sobriety.

TO THE NEWCOMER: It is your life. It is your choice. If you are not completely convinced to your own satisfaction that you are an alcoholic, that your life has become unmanageable; if you are not ready to part with alcohol forever, it would be better for all concerned if you discontinue reading this and give up the idea of becoming a member of Alcoholics Anonymous.

For if you are not convinced, it is not only wasting your own time, but the time of scores of men and women who are genuinely interested in helping you.

II - TO THE LADIES: If we seem to slight you in this booklet it is not intentional. We merely use the masculine pronouns "he" and "him" for convenience. We fully realize that alcohol shows no partiality. It does not respect age, sex, nor estate. The millionaire drunk on the best Scotch and the poor man drunk on the cheapest rotgut look like twin brothers when they are in a hospital bed or the gutter. The only difference between a female and a male drunk is that the former is likely to be treated with a little more consideration and courtesy - although generally she does not deserve it. Every word in this pamphlet applies to women as well as men. - THE EDITORS.

III - A WORD TO THE SPONSOR who is putting his first newcomer into a hospital or otherwise introducing him to this new way of life: You must assume full responsibility for this man. He trusts you, otherwise he would not submit to hospitalization. You must fulfill all pledges you make to him, either tangible or intangible. If you cannot fulfill a promise, do not make it. It is easy enough to promise a man that he will get his job back if he sobers up. But unless you are certain that it can be fulfilled, don't make that promise. Don't promise financial aid unless you are ready to fulfill your part of the bargain. If you don't know how he is going to pay his hospital bill, don't put him in the hospital unless you are willing to assume financial responsibility.

It is definitely your job to see that he has visitors, and you must visit him frequently yourself. If you hospitalize a man and then neglect him, he will naturally lose confidence in you, assume a "nobody loves me" attitude, and your half-hearted labors will be lost.

This is a very critical time in his life. He looks to you for courage, hope, comfort and guidance. He fears the past. He is uncertain of the future. And he is in a frame of mind that the least neglect on your part will fill him with resentment and self-pity. You have in your hands the most valuable property in the world - the future of a fellow man. Treat his life as carefully as you would your own. You are literally responsible for his life.

Above all, don't coerce him into a hospital. Don't get him drunk and then throw him in while he is semi-conscious Chances are he will waken wondering where he is, how he got there. And he won't last.

You should be able to judge if a man is sincere in his desire to quit drinking. Use this judgment. Otherwise you will find yourself needlessly bumping your head into a stone wall and wondering why your "babies" don't stay sober. Remember your own experience. You can remember many times when you would have done anything to get over that awful alcoholic sickness, although you had no desire in the world to give up drinking for good. It doesn't take much good health to inspire an alcoholic to go back and repeat the acts that made him sick. Men who have had pneumonia don't often wittingly expose themselves a second time. But an alcoholic will deliberately get sick over and over again with brief interludes of good health.

You should make it a point to supply your patient with the proper literature - the big "Alcoholics Anonymous" book, this pamphlet, other available pamphlets, a Bible, and anything else that has helped you. Impress upon him the wisdom and necessity of reading and rereading this literature. The more he learns about A.A., the easier the road to sobriety.

Study the newcomer and decide who among your A.A. friends, might have the best story and exert the best influence on him. There are all types in A.A. and regardless of whom you hospitalize; there are dozens who can help him. An hour on the telephone will produce callers. Don't depend on chance. Stray visitors may drop in, but twenty or thirty phone calls will clinch matters and remove uncertainty. It is your responsibility to conjure up callers.

Impress upon your patient that his visitors are not making purely social calls. Their conversation is similar to medicine. Urge him to listen carefully to all that is said, and then meditate upon it after his visitor leaves.

When your patient is out of the hospital your work has not ended. It is now your duty not only to him but to yourself to see that he starts out on the right foot.

Accompany him to his first meeting. Take him along with you when you call on the next patient. Telephone him when there are other patients. Drop in at his home occasionally. Telephone him as often as possible. Urge him to look up the new friends he has made. Counsel and advise him. There was a certain amount of glamour connected with being a patient in the hospital. He had many visitors. His time was occupied. Out now that he has been discharged, the glamour has worn off. He probably will be lonely. He may be too timid to seek the companionship of his new friends.

Experience has proved this to be a very critical period. So your labors have not ended. Give him as much attention as you did when you first called on him - until he can find the road by himself.

Remember, you depend on the newcomer to keep you sober as much as he depends on you. So never lose touch with your responsibility, which never ends.

Remember the old adage, "Two is company and three is a crowd." If you find a patient has one or more visitors don't go into the room. An alcoholic goes to the hospital for two reasons only - to get sober and to learn how to keep sober. The former is easy. Cut off the alcohol and a person is bound to get sober. So the really important thing is to learn how to keep sober. Experience has taught that when more than three gather in a room, patient included, the talk turns to the World Series, politics, funny drunken incidents, and "I could drink more than you."

Such discussion is a waste of the patient time and money. It is assumed that he wants to know how you are managing to keep sober, and you won't hold his attention if there is a crowd in the room.

If you must enter the room when there is another visitor, do it quietly and unobtrusively. Sit down in a corner and be silent until the other visitor has concluded. If he wants any comments from you he will ask for them.

One more word. It is desirable that the patient's visitors be confined to members of Alcoholics Anonymous. Have a quiet talk with his wife or his family before he goes to the hospital. Explain that he will be in good hands and that it is only through kindness to him that his family and friends are asked to stay away. New members are likely to be a little shy. If they find a woman in the patient's room they are not inclined to "let down their hair." The older hands don't mind it, but a new member might unwittingly be kept from delivering a valuable message.

IV - TO THE NEWCOMER: Now you are in the hospital. Or perhaps you are learning to be an Alcoholic Anonymous the "hard way" by continuing at your job while undertaking sobriety.

You will have many callers. They will come singly and in pairs. They may arrive at all hours, from early morning to late night. Some you will like; some you will resent some will seem stupid; others will strike you as silly, fanatic or slightly insane; some will tell you a story that will be "right down your alley." But remember this - never for one minute forget it:

Every single one of them is a former drunk and every single one is trying to help you! Your visitor has had the very problems that you are facing now. In comparison with some, your problems are trifles. You have one thing in common with every visitor - an alcoholic problem. Your caller may have been sober for a week or for half a decade. He still has an alcoholic problem, and if he for one moment forgets to follow any single rule for sober living, he may be occupying your hospital bed tomorrow.

==Alcoholics Anonymous is one hundred percent effective for those who faithfully follow the rules. It is those who try to cut corners who find themselves back in their old drunken state.==

Your visitor is going out of his way, taking up his time, perhaps missing a pleasant evening at home or at the theater by calling on you. His motives are two-fold: He is selfish in that by calling on you he is taking out a little more "sobriety insurance" for himself; and secondly, he is genuinely anxious to pass along the peace and happiness a new way of life has brought him. He is also paying off a debt - paying the people who led him to the path of sobriety by helping someone else. In a very short time you too will find yourself paying off your debt, by carrying the word to another.

Always bear in mind that your caller not so many days or months ago occupied the same bed you are in today. And here we might, despite our promise earlier in the booklet, give you a hint on the spiritual phase of Alcoholics Anonymous. You will be told to have faith in a Higher Poorer. First have faith in your visitor. He is sincere. He is not lying to you. He is not attempting to sell you a bill of goods. A.A. is given away, not sold. Believe him when he tells you what you must do to attain sobriety.

His very presence and appearance should be proof to you that the A.A. program really works. He is extending a helping hand and for himself asks nothing in return. Regardless of who he is or what he has to say, listen to him carefully and courteously. Your alcohol-befuddled mind may not absorb all he says in an hour's conversation, but you will find that when he leaves certain things he has said will come back to you. Ponder these things carefully they may bring you salvation. It has been the history of A.A. that one never knows where lightning will strike. You may pick up the germ of an idea from the most unexpected source. That single idea may shape the course of your entire life, may be the start of an entirely new philosophy. So no matter who your caller is, or what he says, listen attentively.

Your problem has always seemed to be shared by no one else in this world. You cannot conceive of anyone else in your predicament.

Forget it! Your problem dates back to the very beginning of history. Some long-forgotten hero discovered that the juice of the grape made a pleasant drink that brought pleasant results. That same hero probably drank copiously until he suddenly discovered that he could not control his appetite for the juice of the grape. And then he found himself in the same predicament you are in now - sick, worried, crazed with fear, and extremely thirsty.

Your caller once felt that he alone in the world had a drinking problem, and was amazed into sobriety when he discovered that countless thousands were sharing his troubles.

He also found out that when he brought his troubles out of their dark and secret hiding place and exposed them to the cleansing light of day, they were half conquered. And so it will be for you. Bring your problems out in the open and you will be amazed how they disappear.

It cannot be repeated too often: Listen carefully and think it over at great length.

V - Now You Are Alone. When you go to the hospital with typhoid fever your one thought is to be cured. When you go to the hospital as a chronic alcoholic your only thought should be to conquer a disease that is just as deadly if not so quick to kill. And rest assured that the disease is deadly. The mental hospitals are filled with chronic alcoholics. The vital statistics files in every community are filled with deaths due to acute alcoholism.

This is the most serious moment in your life. You can leave the hospital and resume an alcoholic road to an untimely grave or padded cell, or you can start upward to a life that is happy beyond any expectation.

It is your choice and your choice alone. Your newly found friends cannot police you to keep you sober. They have neither the time nor the inclination. They will go to unbelievable lengths to help you but there is a limit to all things.

Shortly after you leave the hospital you will be on your own. The Bible tells us to put "first things first." Alcohol is obviously the first thing in your life. So concentrate on conquering it.

You could have gone through the mechanics of sobering up at home. Your new friends could have called on you in your own living room. But at home there would have been a hundred and one thing to distract your attention - the radio, the furnace, a broken screen door, a walk to the drug store, your own family affairs. Every one of these things would make you forget the most important thing in your life, the thing upon which depends life of death – complete and endless sobriety. That is why you are in the hospital. You will have time to think; you have time to read; you will have time to examine your life, past and present, and to reflect upon what it can be in the future. And don't be in a hurry to leave. Your sponsor knows best. Stay in the hospital until you have at least a rudimentary understanding of the program.

There is the Bible that you haven't opened for years. Get acquainted with it. Read it with an open mind. You will find things that will amaze you. You will be convinced that certain passages were written with you in mind. Read the Sermon on the Mount (Matthew V, VI, and VII). Read St. Paul's inspired essay on love (I Corinthians XIII). Read the Book of James. Read the Twenty-third and Ninety-first Psalms. These reading are brief but so important. Read "Alcoholics Anonymous" and then read it again. You may find that it contains your own story. It will become your second Bible. Ask your callers to suggest other readings.

And if you are puzzled, ask questions. One of your callers will know the answers. Get your sponsor to explain to you the Twelve Steps. If he is not too certain about them - he may be new in this work - ask someone else. The Twelve Steps are listed in the back of this booklet.

There is no standing still in A.A. You either forge ahead or slip backwards. Even the oldest members, the founders, learn something new almost every day.

You can never learn too much in the search for sobriety.

VI - NOW YOU ARE OUT OF THE HOSPITAL

By this time you should know if you want to go along with A.A., or if you want to slip back into that old headache that you called life. You are physically sober and well -- a bit shaky, perhaps but that will wear off in a short time. Reflect that you didn't get into this condition overnight, and that you cannot expect to get out of it in a couple of hours or days.

You feel good enough to go on another bender, or good enough to try a different scheme of things - sobriety.
You have decided to go along with Alcoholics Anonymous? Very well, you will never regret it. First off, your day will have a new pattern. You will open the day with a quiet period. This will be explained by your sponsor. You will read the "Upper Room," or whatever you think best for yourself. You will say a little prayer asking for help during

the day. You will go about your daily work, and your associates will be surprised at you clear-eyed, the disappearance of that haunted look and your willingness to make up for the past. Your sponsor may drop in to see you, or call you on the telephone. There may be a meeting of an A.A. group. Attend it without question. You have no valid excuse except sickness or being out of town, for not attending. You may call on a new patient. Don't wait until tomorrow to do this. You will find the work fascinating. You will find a kindred soul. And you will be giving yourself a new boost along the road to sobriety. Finally, at the end of the day you will say another little prayer of thanks and gratitude for a day of sobriety. You will have lived a full day - a full, constructive day. And you will be grateful.

You feel that you have nothing to say to a new patient? No story to tell? Nonsense! You have been sober for a day, or for a week. Obviously, you must have done something to stay sober, even for that short length of time. That is your story. And believe it or not, the patient won't realize that you are nearly as much of a novice as he is. Definitely you have something to say. And with each succeeding visit you will find that your story comes easier, that you have more confidence in your ability to be of help. The harder you work at sobriety the easier it is to remain sober.

Your sponsor will take you to your first meeting. You will find it new, but inspirational. You will find an atmosphere of peace and contentment that you didn't know existed

After you have attended several meetings it will be your duty to get up on your feet and say something. You will have something to say, even if it is only to express gratitude to the group for having helped you. Before many months have passed you will be asked to lead a meeting. Don't try to put it off with excuses. It is part of the program. Even if you don't think highly of yourself as a public speaker, remember you are among friends, and that your friends also are ex-drunks.

Get in contact with your new friends. Call them up. Drop in at their homes or offices. The door is always open to a fellow-alcoholic.

Before long you will have a new thrill -- the thrill of helping someone else. There is no greater satisfaction in the world than watching the progress of a new Alcoholic Anonymous. When you first see him in his hospital bed he may be unshaved, bleary-eyed, dirty and incoherent. Perhaps the next day he has shaved and cleaned up. A day later his eyes are brighter, new color has come into his face. He talks more intelligently. He leaves the hospital, goes to work, and buys some new clothes. And in a month you will hardly recognize him as the derelict you first met in the hospital. No whisky in the world can give you this thrill.

Above all, remember this: Keep the rules in mind. As long as you follow them you are on firm ground. But the least deviation - and you are vulnerable.

AS A NEW MEMBER, remember you are one of the most important cogs in the machinery of A.A. Without the work of the new member, A.A. could not have grown as it has. You will bring into this work a fresh enthusiasm, the zeal of a crusader. You will want everyone to share with you the blessings of this new life. You will be tireless in your efforts to help others. And it is a splendid enthusiasm! Cherish it as long as you can.

[As a gentleman by the name of Bob Crisp once said; "Ignorance on Fire, People will come for hundreds of miles to watch this fool burn, who is full of enthusiasm!]
Added by author.

It is not likely that your fresh enthusiasm will last forever. You will find, however, that as initial enthusiasm wanes, it is replaced with a greater understanding, deeper sympathy, and a more complete knowledge. You will eventually become an "elder statesman" of A.A. and you will be able to use your knowledge to help not only brand new members, but those who have been members for a year or more, but who still have perplexing problems. And as a new member, do not hesitate to bring your problems to these "elder statesmen." They may be able to solve your headaches and make easier your path.

And now you are ready to go back and read Part III of this booklet. For you are ready to sponsor some other poor alcoholic who is desperately in need of help, both human and Divine.

So God bless you and keep you.

YARDSTICK FOR ALCOHOLICS

THE PROSPECTIVE MEMBER of A.A. may have some doubts if he is actually an alcoholic. A.A. in Akron has found a yardstick prepared by psychiatrists of Johns Hopkins University to be very valuable in helping the alcoholic decide for himself.

Have your prospect answer the following questions, being as honest as possible with himself in deciding the answers. If he answers Yes to one of the questions, there is a definite warning that he MAY be an alcoholic. If he answers YES to any two, the chances are that he IS an alcoholic. If he answers YES to any three or more, he IS DEFINITELY an alcoholic and in need of help.

The questions:

1. Do you lose time from work due to drinking?
2. Is drinking making your home life unhappy?
3. Do you drink because you are shy with other people?
4. Is drinking affecting your reputation?
5. Have you gotten into financial difficulties as a result of drinking?

6. Have you ever stolen, pawned property, or "borrowed" to get money for alcoholic beverages?
7. Do you turn to lower companions and an inferior environment when drinking?
8. Does your drinking make you careless of your family's welfare?
9. Has your ambition decreased since drinking?
10. Do you crave a drink at a definite time daily?
11. Do you want a drink the next morning?
12. Does drinking cause you to have difficulty in sleeping?
13. Has your efficiency decreased since drinking?
14. Is drinking jeopardizing your job or business?
15. Do you drink to escape from worries or troubles?
16. Do you drink alone?
17. Have you ever had a complete loss of memory as a result of drinking?
18. Has your physician ever treated you for drinking?
19. Do you drink to build up your self-confidence?
20. Have you ever been to a hospital or institution on account of drinking?

RANDOM THOUGHTS

NOW THAT YOU ARE SOBER, you naturally feel that you want to make restitution in every possible way for the trouble you have caused your family, your friends - others. You want to get back on the job - if you still have a job - earn money, pay your immediate debts and obligations of long standing and almost forgotten. Money - you must have money, you think. And you also want to make restitution in action in many ways, not financial. If you could wave a magic wand and do all these things you would do it, wouldn't you? Well, don't be in a hurry. You can't do all these things overnight. But you can do them - gradually, step by step. You may safely leave these matters to a Higher Power as you perhaps ponder them in your morning period of contemplation. If you are sincerely resolved to do your part, they will all be adjusted.

"Be still and know that I am God."

SOBRIETY IS THE MOST IMPORTANT THING IN YOUR LIFE, without exception. You may believe your job, or your home life, or one of many other things comes first.

But consider, if you do not get sober and stay sober, chances are you won't have a job, a family, or even sanity or life. If you are convinced that everything in life depends on your sobriety, you have just so much more chance of getting sober and staying sober. If you put other things first you are only hurting your chances.

YOU AREN'T very important in this world. If you lose your job someone better will replace you. If you die your wife will mourn briefly, and then remarry. Your children will grow up and you will be but a memory. In the last analysis, you are the only one who benefits by your sobriety. Seek to cultivate humility. Remember that cockiness leads to a speedy fall.

IF YOU THINK you can cheat - sneak a drink or two without anyone else knowing it - remember, you are only cheating yourself. You are the one who will be hurt by conscience. You are the one who will suffer a hangover. You are the one who will return to a hospital bed.

Bear constantly in mind that you are only one drink away from trouble. Whether you have been sober a day, a month, a year or a decade, one single drink is a certain way to go off on a binge or a series of binges. It is the first drink - not the second, fifth or twentieth, that causes the trouble. Remember, the more A.A. work you do, the harder you train, the less likely it is that you will take that first drink.

It is something like two boxers. If they are of the same weight, the same strength and the same ability, and only one trains faithfully while the other spends his time in night dubs and bars, it is pretty sure that the man who trains will be the winner. So let attendance at meetings be your road work; helping newcomers your sparring and shadow boxing your reading, meditation and clear thinking your gymnasium work and you won't have to fear a knockout at the hands of John Barleycorn.

Take therefore no thought for the morrow: for the morrow shall take thought for the things itself. Sufficient unto the day is the evil thereof. - Matthew VI, 34.

Those words are taken from the Sermon on the Mount. Simply, they mean live in today only. Forget yesterday. Do not anticipate tomorrow. You can only live one day at a time and if you do a good job of that, you will have little trouble. One of the easiest, most practical ways of keeping sober ever devised is the day by day plan - the 24-hour plan.

You know that it is possible to stay sober for 24 hours. You have done it many times. All right, stay sober for one day at a time. When you get up in the morning, make up your mind that you will not take a drink for the entire day. Ask the Greater Power for a little help in this. If anyone asks you to have a drink, take a rain check. Say you will have it tomorrow. Then when you go to bed at night, finding yourself sober, say a little word of thanks to the Greater Power for having helped you.

Repeat the performance the next day, and the next day. Before you realize it you will have been sober a week, a month, a year. And yet you have only been sober a day at a time.

If you set a time limit on your sobriety you will be looking forward to that day, and each day will be a burden to you. You will burn with impatience. But with no goal the whole thing clears itself, almost miraculously.

Try the day by day plan.

Medical Men will tell you that alcoholics are all alike in at least one respect: they are emotionally immature. In other words, alcoholics have not learned to think like adults. The child, lying in bed at night, becomes frightened by a shadow on the wall, and hides his head under the covers.

The adult, seeing the same shadow, knows there is a logical reason for it. He sees the streetlight, then the bedpost, and he knows what causes the shadow. He has simply done what the child is incapable of doing - THOUGHT. And through thinking he has avoided fear.

Learn to think things out. Take a thought and follow it through to its conclusion.

If you are tempted to take a drink, reason out for yourself what will happen. Because if you will give serious consideration to the consequences you will have the battle won.

SO YOU'RE DIFFERENT! So you think you are not an alcoholic!

As many Alcoholics Anonymous have gone off the deep end for that kind of thinking as almost all the other reasons combined.

If you have all the symptoms your sponsor will tell you about and that you hear about at meetings, rest assured you are an alcoholic and no different from the rest of the breed.

But don't make the mistake of finding it out the hard way - by experimenting with liquor. You will find it a painful experience and will only learn that you are NOT different.

AT MEETINGS don't criticize the leader. He has his own problems and is doing his best to solve them. Help him along by standing up and saying a few words. He will appreciate your kindness and thoughtfulness.

DON'T criticize the methods of others. Strangely enough, you may change your own ideas as you become older in sobriety. Remember there are a dozen roads from New York to Chicago, but they all land in Chicago

WHAT'S YOUR HURRY? Perhaps you don't feel you are getting the hang of this program as rapidly as you should. Forget it. It probably took you years to get in this condition. You certainly cannot expect a complete cure overnight. You are not expected to grasp the entire program in one day. No one else has ever done that, so it certainly is not expected of you. Even the earliest members are learning something new about sober living nearly every day. There is an old saying, "Easy does it." It is a motto that any alcoholic could well ponder. A child learns to add and subtract in the lower grades. He is not expected to do problems in algebra until he is in high school. Sobriety is a thing that must be learned step by step. If anything puzzles you, ask your new friends about it, or forget it for the time being. The time is not so far away when you will have a good understanding of the entire program. Meantime, EASY DOES IT!

THE A.A. PROGRAM is not a "cure," in the accepted sense of the word. There is no known "cure" for alcoholism except complete abstinence. It has been definitely proved that an alcoholic can never again be a normal drinker. The disease, however, can be arrested. How soon you will be cured of a desire to drink is another matter. That depends entirely upon how quickly you can succeed in changing your fundamental outlook on life. For as your outlook changes for the better, desire will become less pronounced, until it disappears almost entirely. It may be weeks or it may be months. Your sincerity and your capacity for working with others on the A.A. program will determine the length of time.

Earlier in this pamphlet it was advised to keep relatives away from the hospital. The reason was explained. But after the patient leaves the hospital, it would be advisable to bring the wife, husband, or other close relative to meeting. It will give them a clearer understanding of the program and enable them to cooperate more intelligently and more closely in the period of readjustment.

DIET AND REST AND PLAY an important part in the rehabilitation of an alcoholic. For many we bludgeoned ourselves physically, eating improper foods, sleeping with the aid of alcohol. In our drinking days we ate a bowl of chili or a hamburger sandwich because they were filling and cheap. We sacrificed good food so we would have more money for whiskey. We were the living counterparts of the old joke: "What, buying bread? And not a drop of whiskey in the house!" Our rest was the same. We slept when we passed out. We were the ones who turned out the streetlights and rolled up the sidewalks.

We now find that it is wise to eat balanced meals at regular hours, and get the proper amount of sleep without the unhealthy aid of liquor and sleeping pills. Vitamin B1 (Thiamin Hydrochloride) or B Complex will help steady our nerves and build up a vitamin deficiency. Fresh vegetables and fruits will help.

In fact, it is a wise move to consult a physician, possibly have a complete physical examination. Your doctor then will recommend a course in vitamins, a balanced diet, and advise you as to rest.

The reason for this advice is simple. If we are undernourished and lack rest we become irritable and nervous. In this condition our tempers get out of control, our feelings are easily wounded and we get back to the old and dangerous thought processes - "Oh, to Hell with it. I'll get drunk and show 'em."

MANY MEMBERS of A.A. find it helpful, even after a long period of sobriety, to add an extra ration of carbohydrates to their diet. Alcohol turns into sugar in the body, and when we deprive ourselves of alcohol our bodies cry for sugar. This often manifests itself in a form of nervousness.

Carry candy in your pocket. Keep it in your home. Eat deserts. Try an occasional ice cream soda or malted milk. You may find that it solves a problem by calming your nerves.

MEETINGS

IT HAS BEEN found advisable to hold meetings at least once a week at a specified time and place. Meetings provide a means for an exchange of ideas, the renewing of friendships, opportunity to review the work being carried on, a sense of security, and an additional reminder that we are alcoholics and must be continuously on the alert against the temptation to slip backward into the old drunken way of living.

In larger communities where there are several groups it is recommended that the new member attend as many meetings as possible. He will find that the more he is exposed to A.A. the sooner he will absorb its principles, the easier it will become to remain sober, and the sooner problems will shrink and tend to disappear.

As a newcomer you will be somewhat bewildered by your first meeting. It is even possible that it will not make sense to you. Many have this experience. But if you don't find yourself enjoying your first meeting, pause to remember that you probably didn't care for the taste of your first drink of whisky - particularly if it was in bootleg days.

Again, you may feel like a "country cousin" at your first meeting. Your sponsor should see to it that this is not the case. But even if he neglects his duty, don't feel too badly. Don't be afraid to "horn in." If you are being neglected it is just an oversight, and you are entirely welcome. It is possible that you may not even be recognized because your appearance has changed for the better. In a week or two you will find yourself in the middle of things - and very likely neglecting other newcomers.

So attend your first meeting with an open mind. Even if you aren't impressed try it again. Before long you will genuinely enjoy attending and a little later you will feel that the week has been incomplete if you have not attended at least one A.A. meeting. Remember that attendance at meetings is one of the most important requisites of remaining sober.

A.A. OF AKRON gets many inquiries about how to conduct a meeting. Methods differ in many parts of the country. There are discussion groups, study groups, meeting where a leader takes up the entire time himself, etc.

Here, briefly, is how meetings are conducted in the dozen or more Akron groups, a method that has been used since the founding of A.A.: The speaker can be selected from the local group, someone from another group or another city, or on occasion, a guest from the ranks of clergymen, doctor, the judiciary, or anyone who may be of help. In the case of such an outsider, he is generally introduced by the secretary or some other member.

The leader opens the meeting with a prayer, or asks someone else to pray. The prayer can be original, or it can be taken from a prayer book, or from some publication such as "The Upper Room."

The topic is entirely up to the leader. He can tell of his drinking experiences, or what he has done to keep sober, or he can advance his own theories on A.A. His talk lasts from 20 to 40 minutes, at which time he asks for comment or testimony from the floor.

Just before the meeting closes - one hour in Akron - the leader asks for announcements or reports (such as next week's leader, social affairs, new members to be called on, etc.). In closing the entire group stands and repeats the Lord's Prayer. It is courteous to give the speaker enough advance notice so that he may prepare his talk if he so desires.

The Physical set-up of groups varies in many cities. Those who are about to start new groups may be interested in the method used by Akron Group No 1. It is merely a suggestion, however.

When there are but very few members it is customary to hold the meetings in private homes of the members, on the same night of each week. When the group becomes larger, however, it is desirable to hold the meeting in a regular place. A school room, a room in a Y. M.C. A. or lodge, or hotel will do.

It has been the experience throughout the country that the more fluid the structure of the group the more successful the operation.

Akron Group No. 1 has a very simple set-up. There is a permanent secretary, who makes announcements, keeps a list of the membership, and takes care of correspondence. There is also a permanent treasurer, who takes care of the money and pays bills. Then there is a rotating committee of three members to take care of current affairs. Each member serves for three months, but a new one is added and one dropped every month. This committee takes care of providing leaders, supplying refreshments, arranging parties, greeting newcomers, etc.

[On the topic of Service work; my book tells me the **Primary Purpose** *is to carry the message, which is the program of recovery, to the Newcomer.* Every other aspect of service work is Icing on the Cake. In order to carry the message you must have worked the steps and have a working knowledge of the Big Book. It is just like baking a cake you must follow the instructions to produce a cake…then you can put the icing on it. You don't take two weeks to bake a cake consequently you don't take months to work the steps. I take new people thru the steps in 12 to 14 days. During that time, they also worked the steps. They are then out there carrying the message of recovery.] SantaC.

As the group grows older certain qualifications, in terms of length of sobriety, can be made. Akron Group No. 1 requires a full year of continuous sobriety as qualification to hold an office or serve.

There are no dues. There is a free-will offering at each meeting to take care of expenses.

There is probably an older group in some community within easy traveling distance of yours. Someone from that group will doubtless be happy to help you get started.

THE TWELVE STEPS

Alcoholics Anonymous is based on a set of laws known as the Twelve Steps. Years of experience have definitely proved that those who live up to these rules remain sober. Those who gloss over or ignore any one rule are in constant danger of returning to a life of drunkenness. Thousands of words could be written on each rule. Lack of space prevents, so they are merely listed here. It is suggested that they be explained by the sponsor. If he cannot explain them he should provide someone who can.

THE TWELVE STEPS

1. We admitted we were powerless over alcohol –that our lives had become unmanageable.
2. Came to believe that a Power greater than ourselves could restore us to sanity.
3. Made a decision to turn our will and our lives over to the care of God as we understood Him.
4. Made a searching and fearless moral inventory of ourselves.

5. Admitted to God, to ourselves, and to another human being the exact nature of our wrongs.
6. Were entirely ready to have God remove all these defects of character.
7. Humbly asked Him to remove our shortcomings.
8. Made a list of all persons we had harmed, and became willing to make amends to them all.
9. Made direct amends to such people wherever possible, except when to do so would injure them or others.
10. Continued to take personal inventory and when we were wrong promptly admitted it.
11. Sought through prayer and meditation to improve our conscious contact with God as we understood Him, praying only for knowledge of His will for us and the power to carry that out.
12. Having had a spiritual awakening as the result of these steps, we tried to carry this message to alcoholics, and to practice these principles in all our affairs.

SUGGESTED READING

The following literature has helped many members of Alcoholics Anonymous.

Alcoholics Anonymous. (Works Publishing Company.)

The Holy Bible.

The Greatest Thing in the World. Henry Drummond.

The Unchanging Friend. (A Series) (Bruce Publishing Co., Milwaukee.)

As a Man Thinketh. James Allen.

The Sermon on the Mount. Emmet Fox (Harper Bros.)

The Self You Have to Live With. Winfred Rhoades. (Lippincott.)

Psychology of Christian Personality. Ernest M. Ligon. (Macmillan Co.)

Abundant Living. E. Stanley Jones

The Man Nobody Knows. Bruce Barron

(Editor's Note, 1997: Some of the above books are still in print, especially The Sermon on The Mount, and of course, The Big Book and the Bible. I have located a few of them in used bookstores.)

This pamphlet is no longer in print or available from Group No. 1, although Group No. 1 is still active in Akron.

"A Manual for Alcoholics Anonymous", written and distributed in 1940 by Dr. Bob's Home Group, A.A. Group No. 1, Akron, Ohio.

Dr. Bob (one of our co-founders) probably wrote or heavily influenced the writing and distribution of this pamphlet. Dr. Bob was the Prince of 12 Steppers, from the day he achieved permanent sobriety, June 10, 1935, the founding date of Alcoholics Anonymous, until his death, November 16, 1950, carrying the message of A.A. to well over 5000 men and women alcoholics, and to all these he gave his medical services and time without thought of charge.

It is my hope that by getting back to the basics of A.A., and the sharing of this data, that the transition from the life of a drunk to a SOBER LIFE in the program of A.A. will be eased for newcomers.

This pamphlet was written and being distributed within one year of the publication of the Big Book, and the longest sobriety of the "Old Timers" (Bill W.) was only a little over 5 years. A.A. was only 4 1/2 years from its inception and the day of Dr. Bob's last drink. There were only about 800 members of A.A. at the beginning of 1940, nationwide, and almost none in other countries. By the end of 1940 membership had blossomed to about 2000 and by the end of 1941 the membership had skyrocketed to 8000. Today we number in the millions and groups of Sober Alcoholics can be found everywhere in every country throughout the world. Untold millions have found lived and are living a sober life in the 77 years since Ebby first carried a message of hope to Bill W., a desperate, incomprehensibly demoralized drunk.

We can see in our own lives what the efforts of a few relative newcomers has done for us and the world, to remind us to not stint in our efforts so that greater things will come to pass.... To those "newcomers" we owe so much.

THE SPECIFICS OF WHAT THE FOUNDERS DID IN AKRON

First, they would locate a "real" alcoholic who needed help, want help, and would do whatever was expected of him: (Note the sober alcoholic went searching for someone to work with.). In the case of each of the first three A.A.'s -- -Bill Wilson, Dr. Bob Smith, and Bill Dotson--- someone had actually gone searching for each of those three men as "pigeons/babies/sponsees" needing help. Later, wives and relatives would sometimes bring a new man to Dr. Bob for help. Sometimes drunks appeared on the scene and asked for help. But searching out and "qualifying" the new person as one who was serious and willing to go to any length to get well. And that very outreach itself contributed mightily both to the newcomer's possible success and to the continued sobriety of his messenger-helper. All learned in those experiences that you can't make a drunk quit unless he wants to; but you can provide him with a personal testimony of success that has clout and compelling attraction.

WHAT DOES A SPONSOR DO?

If you are looking to become a sponsor please review the following information so you can get a clear understanding of the roles in the sponsor/sponsee relationship.

A brief history of sponsorship: The idea of sponsorship was born in A.A., the original 12 step fellowship. The book "Living Sober" an A.A. publication, describes how the term "sponsor" came about.

In the earliest days of A.A., the term "sponsor" was not in the A.A. jargon. Then a few hospitals in Akron, Ohio and New York began to accept alcoholics (under that diagnosis) as patients -- If a sober A.A. member would agree to "sponsor" the sick man or woman. The sponsor took the patient to the hospital, visited him or her regularly, was present when the patient was discharged, and took the patient home and then to the A.A. meeting. At the meeting, the sponsor introduced the newcomer to other happily non drinking alcoholics. All through the early months of recovery, the sponsor stood by, ready to answer questions, or to listen whenever needed.

Though there are no true references to the word sponsorship with in the first 164 page of the A.A. Big Book "Alcoholics Anonymous" it is mentioned in several of the personal stories that are contained later in the book. *The early history of A.A. tells us that even Bill W. had a sponsor whose name was Edwin T. Thatcher who was born 1896, and died in 1966.*

Bill Wilson was constantly amazed at the growth and apparent success that Cleveland was having in sobering up alcoholics. He visited there every time that he went to Ohio.

Bill later wrote in A.A. Comes of Age: "Yes, Cleveland's results were of the best. Their results were in fact so good, and A.A.'s membership elsewhere was so small, that many a Clevelander really thought A.A.'s membership had started there in the first place. The Cleveland pioneers had proved three essential things: the value of personal sponsorship; the worth of the A.A.'s Big Book in indoctrinating newcomers, and finally the tremendous fact that A.A., when the word really got around, could now soundly grow to great size.

Clarence was a dynamo. He wanted the best for himself and "his boys" in A.A. He refined the art of A.A. sponsorship to the point that Nell Wing, Bill Wilson's secretary, commented to the author that *Clarence was probably the "one man responsible for sponsorship as we know it today."* Sponsorship has since become one of the foundations of the recovery programs for of all the 12 step fellowships and one of the greatest blessings of membership. With it we can help one another to succeed and arrest the disease called addiction one day at a time regardless of the nature.

So just what does a sponsor do?

In some ways, a sponsor is like a:

good friend

teacher

tutor

experienced guide

older brother/sister

A sponsor is someone who has been where we want to go in our twelve step program and knows how we can best get there. Their primary responsibility is to help us work the 12 steps by applying the principles of the program to our lives.

They lead us by example as we see how the program works in their lives through sharing their personal experiences and stories of where they were and where they are now. We start to learn how to become sober by listening and doing the footwork that our sponsor shows us on a daily basis. In time we make these new changes a habit which helps us to remain sober one day at a time.

A.A. defines a sponsorship in this way: "An alcoholic who has made some progress in the recovery program who shares that experience on a continuous, individual basis with another who is attempting to attain or maintain sobriety through A.A."

It is the sponsor's job to help the newcomer become dependent on God and independent or free from the sponsor as quickly as feasible. The sponsor is not a nurse maid, banker, baby sitter, counselor, matchmaker, employment counselor or lawyer. Their primary purpose is to teach you how to take the steps and to navigate the Big Book, Alcoholics Anonymous, and to teach another new person how to do the same.

With that, let's find out how to carry the message.

APPROACHING THE NEWCOMER

One way to do it…

The meeting has ended and you have identified a new comer that you want to talk to because they identified themselves at the beginning of the meeting.

'Hello, my name is _____, glad to meet you _____.

What did you think of the meeting? Wait for answer…

How did you find out about us? Wait for answer…

Do you think you are an Alcoholic?

1) No… OK well if you ever do become one and you want some help, I can help you and give them your Phone number for later…

2) "I don't know"… Go to Pg. 44, B/B; have you ever gone out drinking and said to yourself, I'm going to only drink

(X) amount of drinks and you went way past that number? Have you done that more than once? You're half way there.

3) Have you ever woke up in the morning after one of those times and said to Yourself, I'm never going to do that again and did it again? Bingo you qualify to be a Real Alcoholic.

> *If at any time they say No… Politely thank them and Move on to another newcomer.*

If they identify themselves as Alcoholic, ask them if they would like to do something about it? Would they like to be Recovered Alcoholic instead of a Practicing One?

> *If they answer NO… Politely thank them and move on to another newcomer.*

> *If they answer YES, go to the very 'First page' of your Big Book and read the hand written annotation, you've inserted in your Big Book:*

<u>"You must agree to do everything this book tells us to do? You must engage in the process exactly as it is outlined in</u>

<u>this book."</u> ["*How To Color Your Big Book,*" *audio soon to be published*]

> *If they answer YES, then ask the question:*
> (Trick Question)

<u>If the book says that you have to run down 'Interstate Highway 5' (or any major road in your area) at 4:30 pm to 6:30 PM, You'll do that ? Right ?</u>

> *If they say NO, tell them that they are not ready, but when they are to please call and you and you can help them. (give them your phone number)*
>
> *If they say YES, then you tell them* **great**, *it doesn't say that but if it did they would be butt naked and running.*

Tell them you need to ask them some more questions and it will take about 30 minutes. Do they have enough time to do that? If they don't, be sure to get their phone number and it is your responsibility to call them to set up a time to go over the next part.

At this time you will take them through the twelve steps verbally, giving examples and simple explanations for each step. You don't want anyone saying: "You didn't say that." Or "We never talked about that."

1) We have now established that you are an Alcoholic so let me ask you this: we know that you are powerless over Alcohol, because you drink more than you wanted to and you did stuff that you said you wouldn't do. Isn't that correct? A Yes is required!

2) Do you have a religious background? Do you believe in or practice some Faith? Yes move on to step three. If they answer No, <u>ask them if they would believe that you believe in a Higher Power (God) greater than themselves?</u> Yes move on to step three.

3) Would they be willing to ask this Higher Power (God) to help them make decisions essential to running their lives as outlined in the Big Book, so they could be recovered from this disease? A Yes is required!

4) Now every business that is successful has to take an inventory. They have to look at their liabilities and assets. Would you be willing to look at your liabilities, in the Big Book we call them short comings and defects of character. Would you be willing to identify these liabilities? A Yes is required!

5) Now in business the owners usually go over this list with their accountant, lawyer or a business consultant. Would you be willing to do that with me, a Priest, Minister, Rabbi, counselor, Psychologist, Psychiatrist or even a stranger? Now I would hope that you would do this with me so I could give you feedback on what you have done and coach you if you have left anything out. A Yes is required!

6) Now that you have identified these liabilities would you be willing to have this Higher Power (God) to remove these shortcomings and defects of character, one and all? A Yes is required!

7) Would you ask God to remove these liabilities? A Yes is required!

8) Now you have made a list of shortcomings, so would you be willing to transfer the people from that list to a new list and alongside of them would you specifically identify the amends you feel need to be made? A Yes is required!

9) Now this is difficult to say at this time, but when you have gotten to this point would you be willing to go and make direct amends to those individuals on the new list you have made addressing the amends you have listed and asking them what they need to have a level playing field? *Remember that you and your Sponsor have gone over this list together before you meet these individuals.* A Yes is required!

You have now cleaned up the wreckage of your past. You need not return there again unless it would be beneficial sharing parts that would be beneficial for the newcomer you are working with. The next steps, maintenance steps, help you keep today clean…

10) Would you be willing to clean up the messes that you make today and ask for help in not making anymore?

Another words; <u>Follow Gods Will in your life.</u> A Yes is required!

11) Would you be willing to ask for help in increasing your Spiritual awareness through prayer and meditation and ask God to guide you throughout the day? A Yes is required!

12) And this is the most important part. Would you be willing to pass this on to someone else when you have finished? A Yes is required!

If at anytime they say NO, you stop and tell them that you <u>CANNOT</u> work with them. You can only work with someone who is willing to do the whole thing with No reservations. If at any time later they wish to change their mind you or one of the people you are working with now will be willing to help them.

Please, this is a guide, put it in your own words, but cover all the bases… You only want to work with those who are willing to do the work!!!

Now for Re-treads…Slippers, Bouncers and such. On their first day back ask them if they really want to get Sober and if so are they willing to do what is necessary to do that? Tell them that they are to erase their minds of everything that they thought they knew from previous times, and begin anew. I use the example of the white magic boards that can be erased with a cloth easily. They are to wipe it clean before we begin.

If they agree to that then take them from the top of the page through step 12… after they have agreed to all…. Take both the newcomer and slipper through the Big Book… highlighting, underlining and annotating… upon completion of the Big Book launch them into their Fourth (4th) Step… it should take no longer than ten to 12 (10-12) days to finish the steps and the highlighting and annotating of the Big Book (Expanded print) I am working on an audio CD: "How to Color Your Big Book."

When in a meeting (during this period) they can only say their "Name, I have a Sponsor and I am working the steps" until they have reach the Ninth (9th) Step and are well into the amends part.

In addition, if a newcomer comes to the meeting, they are to introduce themselves and begin to go through the questions with this new individual and bringing them up to where they are in the process. If this is done right they will be ahead of their newcomer and will be carrying the message as they are learning the message themselves.

Before and after the meetings they are welcome to share anything with anyone about where they are in the process and their past. Just NO Sharing during the Meetings until they have something to share about How to be **Recovered**. Meaning they know how to take the steps, have taken them, and can navigate the Big book.

THE ABILITY TO LISTEN CORRECTLY

"Daddy, where did I come from?" the eight-year-old asked.

It was a moment for which her parents had carefully prepared. They took her into the living room, got out the encyclopedia and several other books, and explained all they thought she should know about sexual attraction, affection, love, and reproductions.

Then they both sat back and smiled contentedly.

"Does that answer your question?" her father asked.

"Not really," the little girl said. "Marcia said she came from Detroit. I want to know where I came from."

As a sponsor you will be required to use a trait called active listening. You are putting yourself in the other person's shoes. Figuring out what the real question or meaning is and what they are really asking or saying.

Don't try to answer a question that has not been asked!

GOING THROUGH THE STEPS WITH A SPONSEE

As it was done in the beginning

Before beginning the steps the sponsor must first qualify the person who has requested to follow the path. Find out if they really are alcoholic and, just as important, if YOU feel that they willing and ready to go to any lengths to change their lives and not drink forever. (Page 142, Big Book: "Will he take every necessary step; submit to anything to get well, to stop drinking forever?")

Ask your prospect three qualifying questions:

(1) Do you think you have a drinking problem?
(2) Do you want to do anything about the problem?
(3) What are you willing to do about it?

If you get the answers: (1) yes, (2) yes, and (3) anything, and you feel that the person is ready to follow directions without question, you both are ready to continue all the way. If you feel that they are not ready, tell them so and go on to the next person. (Page 96, Big Book: "To spend too much time on any one situation is to deny some other alcoholic an opportunity to live and be happy.") The program and your own recovery are not dependent upon winning friends and influencing people.

If you feel that they are ready, then you start. There are five phases to the Steps:

1. STEP 1: ADMISSION,
2. STEPS 2 and 3: SUBMISSION,
3. STEPS 4, 5, 6, and 7: CONFESSION,
4. STEPS 8 and 9: RESTITUTION,
5. STEPS 10, 11 and 12: THE LIVING STEPS, CONSTRUCTION AND MAINTENANCE

STEP ONE: Whose boss -- them or the alcohol? (The above qualification should pretty much answer the first half of the step)...That our lives had become unmanageable, not only our drinking -- all phases of our existence were and are unmanageable. It stands to reason that if we can't manage our lives and we are acting in a manner that is not very sane (unmanageability is not sane living) then we have to take...

STEP TWO: Come to believe that a power GREATER than ourselves, something other than us can manage our lives. A power that can bring sanity back to the way we live. Who are we to believe that WE are the greatest? When we did Step 1, we admitted that we couldn't manage our own lives. When we took Step 2, we said that someone greater than us could manage us and restore us. We needed to have a new manager, a living, loving God.

STEP THREE: We made the decision that we needed to come under new management since our own management got us nowhere. So we turn our wills and lives over to the care of our new manager -- God. He will take care of us and manage our lives since we admitted in Step 1 that our lives were unmanageable, and in Step 2, that He could restore us to a manageable state and sanity. At this point both of you get down on your knees... Both on knees, the sponsor says: "God, this is ____(name)____ , he is coming to You in all humility to ask You to guide and direct him. ___(name)___ , realizes that his life is messed up and unmanageable.

__(name)__ is coming to You in all humility to ask to be one of your children -- to work for you, to serve and dedicate his life to You and to turn his will and life over that he may be an instrument of Your love.

Sponsee repeats after sponsor: "God, I ask that You guide and direct me, and that I have decided to turn my will and life over to You. To serve You and dedicate my life to You. I thank you God; I believe that if I ask this in prayer, I shall receive what I have asked for. Thank you, God. Amen."

Now that we have gone under new management, we believe what it says in the Big Book at the end of the Steps in How It Works:

A: We were alcoholic and could not manage our own lives,
B: No human power could RELIEVE our alcoholism,
C: GOD COULD AND WOULD IF HE WERE SOUGHT !!

Then we have to take an inventory.

STEP FOUR: Take a searching and fearless moral inventory. We must find out what we've got, what we need to get rid of, and what we need to acquire. There are some character defects to ask about -- the individual wrongs are not necessary to go over, just the defects that caused them. Going over the questions, you ask that the person be honest and admit his defects to himself, to you, and to God (where two or more are gathered in His name, there shall He be). By admitting, the person also takes:

STEP FIVE: The inventory is of our defects, <u>not our incidents.</u>

Here are the defects:

Resentment, Anger:
Fear, Cowardice:
Self-pity:
Self-justification:
Self-importance, Egotism:
Self-condemnation, Guilt:
Dishonesty:
Hate:
Jealousy:
Laziness:
Insincerity:
Immoral thinking:
Victim:
Making excuses:
Defensive:
Immature:
Defiance:
Lack of respect for others:
Perfectionism, Intolerance:
Wanting responsibility without accountability

Selfishness and self-seeking:
Conceit:
Jealousy:
Sarcasm:
Judgmental:
Lying, Evasiveness,
Impatience:
False pride, Phoniness,
Envy:
Procrastination:
Negative Thinking:
Denial:
Ill-temper:
Will not listen:
Must be right:
Self-centeredness:
Rebellion:
Greed:

Better than or less than (never equal):

Extremist, both positive and negative:

Criticizing, Loose Talk, Gossip:

Inconsiderate (dirty mouth is one)

(The author added more defects than Clarence's original 20)

Now that you've admitted these defects, ask, "Don't you want to get rid of them?" These same defects caused your life to be unmanageable. How can you ask God to get rid of the THINGS you did in your past?

YOU CAN'T!!

You can ask to get rid of the defects, which caused you to act in the manner you did by taking...

STEP SIX: You were ENTIRELY ready (not almost, not just about, not partially) to have God remove ALL (not some) of these defects. He cannot remove things that have already happened. You are ready to get rid of ALL of them, even the ones that are fun. REMEMBER, YOU TURNED YOUR WILL AND LIFE OVER TO GOD IN STEP THREE. Now comes...

STEP SEVEN: On your knees you ask that these defects be removed, these shortcomings listed in your inventory... Both on knees, the sponsor says: "God, here is your child, __(name)__. He is coming to you in all humility to humbly ask your forgiveness, believing that anything he asks in prayer, he humbly shall receive. Person repeats after sponsor: "I, __(name)__, humbly ask you God, to remove my shortcomings and forgive me, my sins and trespasses, and ask in all humility that you will remove my defects and shortcomings because I am one of your children and I truly believe. Thank you God, Amen."

A Prayer For Forgiveness

O loving and kind God, have mercy. Have pity upon me and take away the awful stain of my transgressions. Oh, wash me, cleanse me from this guilt. Let me be pure again. For I admit my shameful deed-it haunts me day and night. It is against you and you alone I sinned and did this terrible thing. You saw it all, and your sentence against me is just. Create in me a new, clean heart, O God, filled with clean thoughts and right desires. Don't toss me aside, banished forever from your presence. Don't take Your Holy Spirit from me. Restore to me again the joy of your salvation, and make me willing to obey you. (***Psalm*** 51:1-12 TLB)

STEP EIGHT: You make a list of all persons you have harmed, starting with yourself, family, friends, employers, employees, etc. We discuss briefly this list, and ask if they are willing to make restitution and amends. (Since the sponsor is boss - you really don't ask... it is assumed.) Then restitution is made to all as soon as possible, except in certain instances where it is turned over to God. You and your sponsor will discuss how you shall make these amends. I have those who I work with make three columns.

Working each column, one at a time; starting with

Column (1) they will list everyone they hold resentments, hurt or owe money too. Don't leave out sex. See page 69 in the BB.

Column (2) what was my part?

Column (3) I have them write out what they need to do to correct it. Then they make an appointment to do the amends. Forgetting their list; they tell the party why they are there and ask what they need to do to make it right. Whatever they are told is what they must do. Even if doesn't seem fair or just.

I've got to remember that I want to clean up my part of the street and do God's will. Nothing happens without his permission. Nothing…

STEP NINE: by making restitution. After doing these 9 steps, your slate is wiped clean. You are reborn as it says in the Big Book on page 63, "We were reborn." (Nobody said I was going to like this; As the Nike commercial says, Just Do It!).

STEP TEN: We continued to take personal inventory every night: Did you harm anyone, have you done something wrong? Do you deserve a gold star or a black mark? You ask forgiveness honestly, and all is forgiven by God -- clean slate. When you are wrong, promptly admit it. When you don't, use the inventory at night to do so. Deal with your life by the four absolutes: ABSOLUTE LOVE, ABSOLUTE HONESTY, ABSOLUTE UNSELFISHNESS, and ABSOLUTE PURITY. Did you act out of Love? Were you honest? Were you unselfish? Were your motives pure? All things must be based on these four things...

Cleaning up the messes is not a destination, it is a journey. I didn't become lily white when I got sober; I just became responsible and accountable for my actions. I can't claim to be a victim…in most circumstance I'm a volunteer.

STEP ELEVEN: Prayer is talking to God -- meditation is listening to Him. Pray, read the Big Book and other spiritual writings including the Bible. Learn the spiritual principles so that you will understand them when you meditate. Remember, **"Thy will, not mine, be done!"**

[There are many books out there, that are not conference approved, that are available to help you widen and give depth to your spiritual life. The old timers read everything they could get their hands on and shared them amongst themselves. It has become a big thing, A.A. approved literature, when in fact there is no A.A. approved literature, what that statement really means is A.A. publishes or prints certain books. If you want to grow spiritually, you must, go outside the walls that have been erected by those who are doing the printing. Look at the percentages recovered in the past compared to those of today and make your decision.] SantaC.

If GOD is the most important person in your life....

How much time do you spend with him ?

STEP TWELVE: A spiritual awakening is THE RESULT of working, DOING, and LIVING, ALL of the 12 Steps! Then you have this message to carry to others. There is no message unless you have done the first 9 Steps and are living in the last three. You can't give away what you don't have. You must practice these principles in ALL your affairs. (The basic outline of these 12 Steps were written by Clarence S. "The Home Brewmeister")

Now it is your responsibility to give this message to others as you have received it. Not changed, watered down, or how others may want it in their lives. If they want what you have, they must do what you did. It is now your legacy to hand down, AS IT WAS GIVEN TO YOU -- NO OTHER WAY!!!! It is recommended that two people work with the newcomer through the steps whenever possible, so that both may learn as well as give.

There is no easier, softer way -- **this is it.** This is the PROGRAM OF RECOVERY as it was in the 1930's and 1940's in Ohio, as Dr. Bob & Clarence S. taught them. You can and DO recover, you don't have to stay sick -- you can and do get WELL!!!

This is the solution; this is HOW IT WORKS.

Don't trudge the Happy Road to Recovery; **Walk with your head high, knowing that through you, God will help others to RECOVER as you have. May God bless and be with you.**

SPONSORSHIP
By Bill W.

"Every sponsor is necessarily a leader. The stakes are huge. A human life, and usually the happiness of a whole family, hangs in the balance. What the sponsor does and says, how well he estimates the reactions of his prospects, how well he times and makes his presentations, how well he handles criticisms, and how well he leads his prospect on by personal spiritual example – well, these attributes of leadership can make all the difference, often the difference between life and death."

I would like my actions to represent the best Big Book that has ever been read but I also must remember that I am not the only copy Big Book out there.

I was taught that the first Nine Steps were to be worked only once and that the only time I revisited them was when it would be beneficial when I worked with a newcomer. In my own life I have worked the first nine steps only once, but I do a daily inventory (Step 10) to clean up the wreckage that I have created today. If something from my past comes up that I didn't list on my original fourth step and it is interfering with my life today, I will handle it on my daily Tenth Step inventory. I write about it, share it with someone and do what is necessary to rectify and clean up the mess. I will search out those involved admit what I have done and ask them what I need to do to make it right. To make a level playing field and seek forgiveness from those involved. Whatever they suggest is what I will do.

The First Drink

A drunk goes in a bar and asks for a shot of Jim Beam. The bartender pours in and the drunk pushes it aside and asks for another shot of Jim Beam. The bartender pours it and the drunk drinks it. The bartender says, "I watched what you did and I don't understand why you pushed the first one away and drank the second one!" The drunk stated, "I've been going to those A.A. meetings, and they said:

WHATEVER YOU DO, DON'T TAKE THAT FIRST DRINK!!!"

UNTREATED ALCOHOLISM - WHO ME?
(SOME QUESTIONS)

Do you have a sponsor?

If yes, what is the EXACT NATURE of the relationship?

If yes, How often do you call (or get together) with him?

What is your idea of an "effective sponsor?"

What is your idea of an "effective sponsee?"

How many A.A. related telephone calls did you receive;

Yesterday?   Last week?   Last month?

How many A.A. related telephone calls did you make;

Yesterday?   Last week?   Last month?

Are you sponsoring any people?

If no, why not?

If yes, how many?

If yes, how often do you get together for that SPECIFIC relationship?

Have you DONE the Steps?

If no, why not?

If yes, how long ago?

How much time did your 4th Step take?

How long, in hours, was your Fifth Step.

Have you held on to some dirty little rotten secret(s)?

Have you HEARD a Fifth Step?

Did you make a Step 8 list?

Have you done your utmost to make AMENDS (vs. "Apologize")

Write a few paragraphs on Step 10.

Do you Pray?   Do You Meditate?

If not, why not?

If so, How often?

Describe the results of your meditation.

Have you had a spiritual awakening?

Describe what you believe to be that experience.

Are you committed to helping others?

Are you a member of a Group?

Do you consider yourself an ACTIVE MEMBER of that Group?

Do you believe that "sober" includes ALL OTHER MIND/MOOD altering drugs?

Do you experience any of the "bedevilment's" described on Page 52 of the *Big Book*?

Having trouble with personal relationships?

Trouble controlling your emotional nature?

Are you a prey to misery?

Are you prone to depression?

Are you having trouble making a living ?

Do you feel useless?

Are you filled with FEAR?

Are you UNHAPPY?

Is your sex life open or secret?

Is it in alignment with your ideals?

DR. BOB'S PRESCRIPTION FOR SOBRIETY

R. H. SMITH, M. D.
2ND NATIONAL BLDG.   AKRON, OHIO
TELEPHONE: HE-8523   REG. NO.

℞ FOR alcoholics
ADDRESS _____ DATE Feb 1937

Always remember it

1. Trust God
2. Clean house
3. Help others

Dr. Bob, M. D.

NR | 1 | 2 | 3 | INF.

The following A.A. Grapevine article was originally published in the November 1968 issue and reprinted in the November 1999 A.A. Grapevine, under the category of "Big Book Authors."

The author of "Home Brewmeister" asserted that in this life-changing program, the growth process never ends.

I'VE NEVER QUIT BEING ACTIVE
by Clarence Snyder
A.A. Grapevine, November 1999

On February 11, 1938, I had my last drink. I was a chronic alky, and through a long, involved miracle, I met my sponsor, Dr. Bob, one of our co-founders. He put me in Akron City Hospital, where I met the alkies who had preceded me in the Fellowship.

Fifteen months later, I organized the Cleveland, Ohio A.A. group. The activity in the Cleveland area was hectic. I spent practically all my time obtaining and following up on publicity for A.A., lining up cooperation with civic and church groups, hospitals, and courts, and helping new groups to start.

So what do I do now, thirty years later? I have never quit being active, although my position in the Fellowship has modified over the years. I attend an average of two meetings per week, when I am home. I am also asked to speak at various groups. In addition, I am invited to take part in numerous group anniversary programs and A.A. roundups around the country (and sometimes out of the country). Many people call upon me for counsel and advice on both personal and group problems. I have an extensive correspondence, since I have made so many friends in A.A. from coast to coast. Once in a while, I sponsor someone. Cases where about everything has been tried, by everyone else, often wind up in my hands.

I have not found the program to be difficult, and I maintain that if it does seem difficult for anyone, he is not doing it "right." Certainly, when I came to this Fellowship, I was in no position or condition to handle anything difficult! I kept things simple. But I must add that when I first began I was well sponsored.

I took measures now summarized in the first nine Steps of the program: admittance of need (the First Step), surrender (Second through Seventh), and restitution (Eighth and Ninth). Having done this, I no longer had a drinking problem, since it had been turned over to a Higher Power. Now I had - and still have - a living problem. But that is taken care of by the practice of Steps Ten, Eleven, and Twelve. So I don't have to be concerned about anything but a simple three-step program, which with practice has become habitual.

Step Ten enables me to check on myself and my activities of the day. I have found that most things disturbing me are little things, but still the very things which, if not dealt with, can pile up and eventually overwhelm me. My daily checkup covers good deeds as well as questionable ones; often, I find I can commend myself in some areas, while in others I owe apologies.

Step Eleven is done after my daily inventory. I usually need the peace resulting from prayer and meditation, and I do receive guidance for my life and actions.

Step Twelve, to me, does involve not only carrying the message, but extending A.A. principles into all phases of my daily life. I learned long ago that this is a life-changing program, but that, after the change occurs, it is necessary for me to go on making the effort to improve myself mentally, morally, and spiritually.

This is my simple program, and I recommend it to anyone who wants a good life and is willing to do his share of helping.

Clarence S., St. Petersburg, Florida

THE PRESCRIPTION

We see so many people in meetings, and out on the streets, still stumbling around with the program, hurting, whining and crying, still all covered up with the Great 3 S's of our disease, Self-pity, Self-righteousness, and Self-Bullshit, and wondering why they can't get **"It"** . . .

In every meeting the **Prescription** is read and heard and referred to, on the walls on posters. It is spelled out precisely in the Big Book on Pages 59 and 60.

Unwilling to disregard fear, and the 7 deadlies mentioned in the 12x12 on page 48, you know, pride, greed, lust, anger, gluttony, envy and **SLOTH**, people trouble themselves in vain to read the teachings. **They see the prescription, but don't take the medicine…. How then can they do away with their illness?"**

From the Big Book Page 72, Chapter 6, INTO ACTION . . .

"In actual practice, we usually find a solitary self-appraisal insufficient. Many of us thought it necessary to go much farther. We will be more reconciled to discussing ourselves with another person when we see good reasons why we should do so. **The best reason first:** If we skip this vital step, we may not overcome drinking. Time after time newcomers have tried to keep to themselves certain facts about their lives. Trying to avoid this humbling experience, they have turned to easier methods. Almost invariably they got drunk. Having persevered with the rest of the program, they wondered why they fell. We think the reason is that they never completed their housecleaning. They took inventory all right, but hung on to some of the worst items in stock. They only *thought* they had lost their egoism and fear; they only *thought* they had humbled themselves. But they had not learned enough of humility, fearlessness and **HONESTY**, in the sense we find it necessary, until they told someone else ALL of their life story.

As it was told to me, "Until someone in A.A. knows everything you know about yourself, you are nowhere."

WHY???

Because, until the steps are done thoroughly, and the

garbage resolved and eliminated, **the old thought system still has a basis for return.** And they still wonder why they are not **Getting "IT"**

"Half-measures availed us nothing!!"

On Page 98 of the Big Book, "Burn the idea into the consciousness of every man [and woman] that he [she] can get well regardless of anyone. The only condition is that he [she] trust in God and clean house."

The Steps of the Program are the Mops and Brooms to Clean House. It isn't any secret, friends, it is all spelled out clearly. **There are 12 things to do, and one to not do, no matter what.**

If the steps are not done, and done thoroughly, then the individual must live with the consequences of that decision or lack of decision . . . **Sorry about that, but that is the way it is, One Day At A Time.** *Barefootsworld (off the net)*

There is another reason people get drunk: They have forgotten they were an alcoholic or they no longer believe they are alcoholic because they stopped doing what works.

APPENDIX I

THE STEPS OF A.A. - AN INTERPRETATION
Written by Clarence H. Snyder, January 1972

Alcoholics Anonymous is not a "booze cure" or a psychological means of controlling one's excessive or obsessive drinking. A.A. is a program, a life changing program, and, in a great part, we owe our inception as a fellowship to our origin in the Oxford Group movement during the mid 1930's.

The Oxford Group was designed as a Life Changing program- and we in A.A. have for our own uses and affiliation, modified their program, chiefly by designing our twelve step program in a manner that the alcoholic who feels he needs and wants a change from what they are experiencing, can comfortably accept and apply the program and thereby change their life.

To do so, requires certain attitudes, willingness, and acts on our parts.

We have simplified the program, in the feeling that any alcoholic with an alcohol problem can live a life free of the obsession to drink.

Our program of the twelve steps is really accepted in four distinct phases, as follows:

1) Need (admission)
2) Surrender (submission)
3) Restitution
4) Construction and Maintenance

Phase #1 - Is covered in Step 1 - "We admitted we were powerless over alcohol, that our lives had become unmanageable" - this step points out phase 1 - or our own need - there is a need for a change!

Phase #2 - Includes the 2nd through the 7th steps which constitutes the phase of submission.

Step #2 - "We came to believe that a power greater than ourselves could restore us to sanity." "Since we could not manage our own lives, of ourselves, we found ourselves to be powerless over alcohol, we were encouraged by the power of example of someone or some others to believe that a power greater than ourselves could restore us to sanity. In this step, we have the "proof of the pudding" before we are asked to eat it!! Others tell us of their experiences and share their deepest feelings with us and those members are alcoholics such as we are, and there they stand, sober, clean-eyed, useful, confident and with a certain radiance we envy and really want for ourselves. So, we *WANT* to believe it! Of course, some persons could conceivably be a bit more startled at first by the reference to "being restored to sanity," but most of us finally conclude that in hearing of some of the experiences our new friends had during their drinking careers were anything but the actions of a rational person, and when we reflect upon our own actions and deeds prior to our own introduction to A.A., it is not difficult to recognize that we too, were pretty well out in left field also! In fact, most of us are happy in the feeling that we were not really responsible for many of our past unpleasant and embarrassing situations and frankly, this step does much to relieve our feelings of guilt and self-condemnation.

Step #3 - "We made a decision to turn our *will and* our *lives* over to the care of God..."

Now here is the step which separates the men from the boys (or the women from the girls) - this is the step which tells the story as to whether we are going to be *in* A.A., or *around* A.A.. Yes, we can attend meetings, visit the clubs, attend the social functions, but, unless we really take step #3, we are continuing to make up our own program. Since our entire program is based upon dependence upon God and our lives are to be directed by Him! So, here we are, making a *decision* which in itself is quite an accomplishment for the alcoholic, since they are one of the most indecisive creatures in society, due to their incapacity to manage their own life due to their obsession- But- to make a decision to turn our life and our will over to the care of God- this creature in the far blue yonder, whom we have little acquaintance with and probably much fear of, this is really asking very, very much of an alcoholic! Rest assured, that if they are not ready, if they have not reached their "bottom" or extremity, and if they are not really "hurting more than they ever have," they are not about to take step #3. So - they go pretty much on their own as usual, except that they do have the advantage of better company than they had been associating with and this in time, could really foul up any type of drinking life they may have in the future! Another important feature enters here, in that they *know* now that there is a way out of their dilemma and this is bound to "work" on them as time goes on, if they have any pride at all in themselves! At this point - their biggest problem is to overcome **FEAR** and "Let go and let God."

Step #4 - "Made a searching and fearless *Moral* inventory of ourselves."

This is a step which should be taken with the assistance of a sponsor, or counselor who is well experienced in this changed life - due to the capacity of the alcoholic to find justification for about anything - a sponsor can bring up through sharing - many various moral weaknesses which need attention in their life and can smooth the way for the alcoholic to examine them in a frank fashion. The next step suggests that someone is helping with step #4 - since it reads as follows:

Step #5 - "Admitted to God, to ourselves, and to *another human being*, the exact *NATURE* of our wrongs."

We put ourselves on record and leave no options nor reservations! Note that it states, *NATURE* of our wrongs- not the wrongs themselves! We are not required to narrate details of our many indiscretions. Many of them we don't even remember, nor are conscious of. This is not a laundry for dirty linen; this is recognition of character defects which need elimination or adjustments!

Step #6 - "Were *entirely* ready to have God remove *ALL* these defects of character."

This step allows for no reservations. The alcoholic, being an extremist must go the whole route. We are not a bit ready, or about to be ready, but *entirely* ready to have God, not us, remove *ALL* these defects of character, (the interesting ones as well as the more damnable ones!).

Step #7 - "Humbly asked Him to remove our shortcomings." We tried to make no deal, as we did in the past when situations would overwhelm us. It was common to say- "Dear God, get me out of this mess and I will be a good boy (or girl), I will not do thus and such, etc., etc., etc.,... " NONE OF THAT! We humbly asked Him to remove our shortcomings. The Good Book assures us that anything we ask believing, we shall receive!

Step #8 - Begins our phase #3- that of restitution. So now we have admission in Step #1, Submission, Steps #2 through #7. Now for the Restitution in Steps #8 and #9.

Step #8 - "Made a list of **all persons** we had harmed and **became willing** to make **amends to them all**. Steps 8 and 9 should also be taken with the assistance of a knowledgeable sponsor or a counselor, since in our present state of impatience with almost complete lack of judgment, we could conceivably cause much harm in executing this phase of the program.

Most of us probably have persons on that list whom we just do not want to have any contact with. The step state plainly - *ALL* persons we had harmed! Obviously some of these persons are not available, having passed on, or disappeared etc., so we must ask God to handle those details.

Step# 9 – But Step #9 states - "Made direct amends *Whenever Possible* except when to do so would injure them or others." We cannot and should not try to clear our slate or conscience at the expense of any others. This phase is very important and it eliminates the possibility of carrying over some details into our new life that could consciously come back to haunt or harm us in our new life. We are going into a new life, and we should "Let the dead bury the dead."

Now that we have taken 9 steps !!! We have concluded 3 phases of our program. These 9 steps we have accomplished - so - FORGET THEM!!! They have required action and you have taken the action, so there is no need of repeating it! There are only two occasions when one must refer back to the first nine steps, #1- is in the event that the person "resigns and resumes," obviously they must start all over again! The other occasion when we may refer to the first nine steps is when we are trying to explain them to a new member and helping them with them.

So, now we have our last phase, that of **Construction;** Steps 10, 11 and 12. With these steps, we construct our life, these are our living steps. We no longer must be concerned with 12 steps- ONLY 3 STEPS!! How simple, how wonderful!!

Step #10 - "Continued to take *personal* inventory, and when we were wrong, promptly admitted it."

This step has absolutely no connection with step #4. Note, in step #4, it calls for a searching and fearless **Moral** inventory. This step calls for a *personal* inventory. This step is our daily check on ourselves. This is our check on the small and large and otherwise details of my life **TODAY**. My simple way of handling step 10 may help someone, since I find that it is most adequate for me, and I prefer to keep things simple and uncomplicated.

At night, after I am in bed, my day is over; I find this is one of my most important prayer times. I think about my day, what have I done, whom I have been with, what has transpired. Sometimes I find that I am not proud of something I have done today, and I owe someone an apology, I do not permit these things to go unattended. I have found that it is not the so-called "big" things which seriously affect the alcoholic in their new life, but the "little" things. They can go on and on and add up and become a real burden and eventually have drastic effects upon our new life. This is the reason for step 10, keep things "cleaned up," keep the walk swept! Maintain a good healthy attitude.

Step #11 - "Sought through Prayer and Meditation, to improve our conscious contact with God, praying *only* for knowledge of His will for us and the power to carry that out."

This is a great step, first, because it brings us into a prayer life. Back in step #3, we made a decision to turn our life and will over to the care of God. In step #11, we receive our orders!! Let us break this step down and discover how it is both simple and profound. We are seeking something, seeking to improve our conscious contact with God. What does that mean? To me it means He is not in the far blue yonder, beyond reach, but right here, close where I can talk to Him and listen to Him (the Bible states that He is closer than hands and feet, and that is most close!). So, I am seeking to make this contact through Prayer and Meditation. What does this mean? To me, Prayer is talking to God, and Meditation is listening to Him! The good Lord endowed us with one mouth and two ears, which should suggest something to us!! We are enjoined- "Be Still" - and that is how we should be while listening! The answers surely will come if we but listen. Now, the step tells us what to pray for. "Only for knowledge of His will for us and the power to carry that out. " Since we submitted ourselves and turned our will and life over to the care of God in phase #2- now we ask for His orders and strength to carry them out. We are promised that He will never expect anything from us that He won't give us the power to execute.

Now then, do you see any place in the step thus far to suggest we pray for sobriety? Of course not, and it is absolutely unnecessary - you *HAVE* sobriety. Thank Him for it - but it is pointless to pray for what you already have The 11th step states very plainly *how to pray* and *what to pray for*!!

Step #12 - We have experienced 11 steps and something has happened to us. In fact, something happened at the end of step 9! Step 12 states very plainly - "Having had a Spiritual Experience as *the* result of these steps, we tried to carry this message to other Alcoholics and to practice these principles in *ALL* of our affairs."

What is a Spiritual Experience? That is the changed life we have been referring to. That is the change that comes to a person who has turned their will over to the care of God and continues to try and improve themselves, mentally, morally and spiritually. It states that we try to carry this message (not the alcoholic) to alcoholics. We practice these principles of love and service in all our affairs. Not just in A.A. meetings and associations, at home, at business, everywhere! What a blessing this fellowship is. What a great opportunity to love and be loved. Why cheat yourself? We have the prescription, the means of getting well, staying well, growing and best of all, *SERVING*. Come on in, the water's fine!! Friends are wonderful, the fellowship is distinct and GOD IS GREAT!!

[This was transcribed from Clarence's handwritten copy.]

APPENDIX II
IMPORTANT ENOUGH TO INCLUDE IN THIS BOOK
(From Volume 1)

THAT AIN'T IN THE BOOK

We hear a lot of stuff said in meetings that can't be reconciled with the program as described in the Big Book of Alcoholics Anonymous. What follows are some of the things we often hear, along with what the Big Book has to say on the subject.

This is a list, along with the corresponding page and paragraph from the Big Book that deals with the subject.

"Remember your last drunk"

Page 24, paragraph 2: "We are unable, at times, to bring into our consciousness with sufficient force the memory of the suffering and humiliation of even a week or a month ago. We are without defense against the first drink."

"I choose not to drink today"

Page 24, paragraph 2: "The fact is that most alcoholics, for reasons yet obscure, have lost the power of choice in drink."

"Play the tape all the way through"

Page 24, paragraph 3: "The almost certain consequences that follow taking even a glass of beer do not crowd into the mind to deter us. If these thoughts do occur, they are hazy and readily supplanted with the old threadbare idea that this time we shall handle ourselves like other people. There is a complete failure of the kind of defense that keeps one from putting his hand on a hot stove."

"Think through the drink"

Page 43, paragraph 4: "Once more: The alcoholic at certain times has no effective mental defense against the first drink. Except in a few rare cases, neither he nor any other human being can provide such a defense. His defense must come from a Higher Power."

"I will always be recovering, never recovered."

Title Page: "ALCOHOLICS ANONYMOUS. The Story of How Many Thousands of Men and Women Have Recovered from Alcoholism."

Page 20, paragraph 2: "Doubtless you are curious to discover how and why, in face of expert opinion to the contrary, we have recovered from a hopeless condition of mind and body."

Page XIII, paragraph 1: "We, of Alcoholics Anonymous, are more than one hundred men and women who have recovered from a seemingly hopeless state of mind and body."

Page 29, paragraph 2: "Further on, clear-cut directions are given showing how we recovered."

Page 132, paragraph 3: "We have recovered, and have been given the power to help others."

"I don't have an alcohol problem, I have a living problem"

Page XXIV, paragraph 2: "In our belief, any picture of the alcoholic which leaves out this physical factor is incomplete."

"Don't drink and go to meetings."

Page 34, paragraph 2: "Many of us felt we had plenty of character. There was a tremendous urge to cease forever. Yet we found it impossible. This is the baffling feature of alcoholism as we know it—this utter inability to leave it alone, no matter how great the necessity or the wish."

Page 34, paragraph 3: "Whether such a person can quit upon a non-spiritual basis depends upon the extent to which he has already lost the power to choose whether he will drink or not."

Page 17, paragraph 2: "Unlike the feelings of the ship's passengers, however, our joy in escape from disaster does not subside as we go our individual ways. The feeling of having shared in a common peril is one element in the powerful cement which binds us. But that in itself would never have held us together as we are now joined."

"This is a selfish program"

Page 20, paragraph 1: "Our very lives, as ex-problem drinkers depend upon our constant thought of others and how we may help meet their needs."

Page 97, paragraph 2: "Helping others is the foundation stone of your recovery. A kindly act once in a while isn't enough. You have to act the Good Samaritan every day, if need be. It may mean the loss of many nights' sleep, great interference with your pleasures, interruptions to your business. It may mean sharing your money and your home, counseling frantic wives and relatives, innumerable trips to police courts, sanitariums, hospitals, jails and asylums. Your telephone may jangle at any time of the day or night."

Page 14-15, paragraph 7: "For if an alcoholic failed to perfect and enlarge his spiritual life through work and self-sacrifice for others, he could not survive the certain trials and low spots ahead."

Page 62, paragraph 2: "Selfishness, self-centeredness! That, we think, is the root of our troubles"

Page 62, paragraph 3: "So our troubles, we think, are basically of our own making. They arise out of ourselves, and the alcoholic is an extreme example of self-will run riot, though he usually doesn't think so. Above everything, we alcoholics must be rid of this selfishness. We must, or it kills us!"

"Meeting makers make it"

Page 59, paragraph 3: "Here are the steps we took, which are suggested as a program of recovery."

"I'm powerless over people, places and things"

Page 132, paragraph 3: "We have recovered, and have been given the power to help others."

Page 122, paragraph 3: "Years of living with an alcoholic is almost sure to make any wife or child neurotic."

Page 82, paragraph 4: "The alcoholic is like a tornado roaring his way through the lives of others. Hearts are broken. Sweet relationships are dead. Affections have been uprooted. Selfish and inconsiderate habits have kept the home in turmoil. We feel a man is unthinking when he says that sobriety is enough."

Page 89, paragraph 2: "You can help when no one else can. You can secure their confidence when others fail."

"You're in the right place"

Page 20-21, paragraph 7: "Then we have a certain type of hard drinker. He may have the habit badly enough to gradually impair him physically and mentally. It may cause him to die a few years before his time. If a sufficiently strong reason - ill health, falling in love, change of environment, or the warning of a doctor - becomes operative, this man can also stop or moderate, although he may find it difficult and troublesome and may even need medical attention."

Page 31, paragraph 2: "If anyone who is showing inability to control his drinking can do the right- about-face and drink like a gentleman, our hats are off to him."

Page 31-32, paragraph 4: "We do not like to pronounce any individual as alcoholic, but you can quickly diagnose yourself. Step over to the nearest barroom and try some controlled drinking. Try to drink and stop abruptly. Try it more than once. It will not take long for you to decide, if you are honest with yourself about it. It may be worth a bad case of jitters if you get a full knowledge of your condition."

Page 108-109, paragraph 6: "Your husband may be only a heavy drinker. His drinking may be constant or it may be heavy only on certain occasions. Perhaps he spends too much money for liquor. It may be slowing him up mentally and physically, but he does not see it. Sometimes he is a source of embarrassment to you and his friends. He is positive he can handle his liquor, that it does him no harm, that drinking is necessary in his business. He would probably be insulted if he were called an alcoholic. This world is full of people like him. Some will moderate or stop altogether, and some will not. Of those who keep on, a good number will become true alcoholics after a while."

Page 92, paragraph 2: "If you are satisfied that he is a real alcoholic"

Page 95, paragraph 4: "If he thinks he can do the job in some other way, or prefers some other spiritual approach, encourage him to follow his own conscience."

"If an alcoholic wants to get sober, nothing you say can make him drink."

Page 103, paragraph 2: "A spirit of intolerance might repel alcoholics whose lives could have been saved, had it not been for such stupidity. We would not even do the cause of temperate drinking any good, for not one drinker in a thousand likes to be told anything about alcohol by one who hates it."

"We must change playmates, playgrounds, and playthings"

Page 100-101, paragraph 5: "Assuming we are spiritually fit, we can do all sorts of things alcoholics are not supposed to do. People have said we must not go where liquor is served; we must not have it in our homes; we must shun friends who drink; we must avoid moving pictures which show drinking scenes; we must not go into bars; our friends must hide their bottles if we go to their houses; we mustn't think or be reminded about alcohol at all. Our experience shows that this is not necessarily so."

"We meet these conditions every day. An alcoholic, who cannot meet them, still has an alcoholic mind; there is something the matter with his spiritual status. His only chance for sobriety would be someplace like the Greenland Ice Cap, and even there an Eskimo might turn up with a bottle of scotch and ruin everything!"

"I'm a people pleaser. I need to learn to take care of myself"

Page 61, paragraph 2: "Is he not really a self-seeker even when trying to be kind?"

"Don't drink, even if your ass falls off."

Page 34, paragraph 2: "Many of us felt we had plenty of character. There was a tremendous urge to cease forever. Yet we found it impossible. This is the baffling feature of alcoholism as we know it—this utter inability to leave it alone, no matter how great the necessity or the wish."

"I haven't had a drink today, so I'm a complete success today."

Page 19, paragraph 1: "The elimination of drinking is but a beginning. A much more important demonstration of our principles lies before us in our respective homes, occupations and affairs."

"It's my opinion that..." or "I don't know anything about the Big Book, but this is the way I do it..."

Page 19, paragraph 1: "We have concluded to publish an anonymous volume setting forth the problem as we see it. We shall bring to the task our combined experience and knowledge. This should suggest a useful program for anyone concerned with a drinking problem."

"Don't drink, no matter what."

Page 34, paragraph 2: "Many of us felt we had plenty of character. There was a tremendous urge to cease forever. Yet we found it impossible. This is the baffling feature of alcoholism as we know it—this utter inability to leave it alone, no matter how great the necessity or the wish."

Page 31, paragraph 4: "We do not like to pronounce any individual as alcoholic, but you can quickly diagnose yourself. Step over to the nearest barroom and try some controlled drinking. Try to drink and stop abruptly. Try it more than once. It will not take long for you to decide, if you are honest with yourself about it. It may be worth a bad case of jitters if you get a full knowledge of your condition."

"We need to give up planning, it doesn't work."

Page 86, paragraphs 3-4: "On awakening let us think about the twenty-four hours ahead. We consider our plans for the day. Before we begin, we ask God to direct our thinking, especially asking that it be divorced from self-pity, dishonest or self-seeking motives. Under these conditions we can employ our mental faculties with assurance, for after all God gave us brains to use. Our thought-life will be placed on a much higher plane when our thinking is cleared of wrong motives. In thinking about our day we may face indecision. We may not be able to determine which course to take. Here we ask God for inspiration, an intuitive thought or a decision. We relax and take it easy. We don't struggle. We are often surprised how the right answers come after we have tried this for a while."

"I have a choice to not drink today."

Page 30, paragraph 3: "We alcoholics are men and women who have lost the ability to control our drinking. We know that no real alcoholic ever recovers control. All of us felt at times that we were regaining control, but such intervals - usually brief - were inevitably followed by still less control, which led in time to pitiful and incomprehensible demoralization. We are convinced to a man that alcoholics of our type are in the grip of a progressive illness. Over any considerable period we get worse, never better."

"If all I do is stay sober today, then it's been a good day."

Page 82, paragraph 3: "Sometimes we hear an alcoholic say that the only thing he needs to do is to keep sober. Certainly he must keep sober, for there will be no home if he doesn't. But he is yet a long way from making good to the wife or parents whom for years he has so shockingly treated."

Page 82 paragraph 4: "We feel a man is unthinking when he says sobriety is enough."

"You don't need a shrink. You have an alcoholic personality. All you will ever need is in the first 164 pages of the Big Book."

Page 133, paragraph 2: "But this does not mean that we disregard human health measures. God has abundantly supplied this world with fine doctors, psychologists, and practitioners of various kinds. Do not hesitate to take your health problems to such persons. Most of them give freely of themselves, that their fellows may enjoy sound minds and bodies. Try to remember that though God has wrought miracles among us, we should never belittle a good doctor or psychiatrist. Their services are often indispensable in treating a newcomer and in following his case afterward."

"A.A. is the only way to stay sober."

page 95, paragraph 4: "If he thinks he can do the job in some other way, or prefers some other spiritual approach, encourage him to follow his own conscience. We have no monopoly on God; we merely have an approach that worked with us."

Page 164, paragraph 3: "Our book is meant to be suggestive only. We realize we know only a little."

"My sponsor told me that, if in making an amends I would be harmed, I could consider myself as one of the 'others' in Step Nine."

Page 79, paragraph 2 "Reminding ourselves that we have decided to go to any lengths to find a spiritual experience, we ask that we be given strength and direction to do the right thing, no matter what the personal consequences might be."

"I need to forgive myself first" or "You need to be good to yourself"

Page 74, paragraph 2: "The rule is we must be hard on our self, but always considerate of others."

"Take what you want and leave the rest"

Page 17, paragraph 3: "The tremendous fact for every one of us is that we have discovered a common solution. We have a way out on which we can absolutely agree, and upon which we can join in brotherly and harmonious action. This is the great news this book carries to those who suffer from alcoholism."

"Just do the next right thing"

Page 86, paragraph 4: "We may not be able to determine which course to take. Here we ask God for inspiration, an intuitive thought or a decision."

Page 87, paragraph 1: " Being still inexperienced and having just made conscious contact with God, it is not probable that we are going to be inspired at all times. We might pay for this presumption in all sorts of absurd actions and ideas."

"Don't make any major decisions for the first year"

Page 60, paragraph 4:
(a) That we were alcoholic and could not manage our own lives.
(b) That probably no human power could have relieved our alcoholism.

(c) That God could and would if He were sought.

Being convinced, we were at Step Three, which is that we decided to turn our will and our life over to God as we understood Him.

Page 76, paragraph 2: "When ready, we say something like this: "My Creator, I am now willing that you should have all of me, good and bad. I pray that you now remove from me every single defect of character which stands in the way of my usefulness to you and my fellows. Grant me strength, as I go out from here, to do your bidding. Amen. " We have then completed Step Seven."

"Stay out of relationships for the first year!"

Page. 69, paragraph 1: "We do not want to be the arbiter of anyone's sex conduct."

Page 69, paragraph 3: "In meditation, we ask God what we should do about each specific matter. The right answer will come if we want it."

Page 69, paragraph 4: "God alone can judge our sex situation."

Page 69-70: "Counsel with other persons is often desirable, but we let God be the final judge."

Page 70, paragraph 2: "We earnestly pray for the right ideal, for guidance in each questionable situation, for sanity, and for the strength to do the right thing."

"Alcohol was my drug of choice"

Page 24, paragraph 2: "The fact is that most alcoholics, for reasons yet obscure, have lost the power of choice in drink."

Page 7, paragraph 1: "A doctor came with a sedative. The next day found me drinking both gin and sedative. This combination soon landed me on the rocks."

Page 22, paragraph 1: "As matters grow worse, he begins to use a combination of high-powered sedative and liquor to quiet his nerves so he could go to work."

"Keep coming back, eventually it will rub off on you"

Page 64, paragraph 1: "Though our decision was a vital and crucial step, it could have little permanent effect unless at once followed by a strenuous effort to face and to be rid of, the things in ourselves which had been blocking us."

"Ninety Meetings in Ninety Days"

Page 15, paragraph 2: "We meet frequently so that newcomers may find the fellowship they seek."

Page 19, paragraph 2: "None of us makes a sole vocation of this work, nor do we think its effectiveness would be increased if we did."

Page 59, paragraph 3: "Here are the steps we took, which are suggested as a program of recovery."

"You only work one step a year" "Take your time to work the steps"

Page 569, paragraph 3: What often takes place in a few months can hardly be brought about by himself alone."

Page 63, paragraph 3: "Next we launched on a course of vigorous action."

Page 74, paragraph 2: "If that is so, this step may be postponed, only, however, if we hold ourselves in complete readiness to go through with it at the first opportunity."

Page 75, paragraph 3: "Returning home we find a place where we can be quiet for AN HOUR, carefully reviewing what we have done."

"Make sure to put something good about yourself in your 4th step inventory."

Page 64 paragraph 3: "First, we searched out the flaws in our make-up which caused our failure."

Page 67 paragraph 3: "The inventory was ours, not the other man's." When we saw our faults we listed them."

Page 71 paragraph 1: "If you have already made a decision, and an inventory of your grosser handicaps, you have made a good beginning."

"You need to stay in those feelings and really feel them."

Page 84, paragraph 2: "When these crop up, we ask God at once to remove them."

Page. 125, paragraph 1: "So we think that unless some good and useful purpose is to be served, past occurrences should not be discussed."

"There are no musts in this program."

Page 99, paragraph 1: "it must be done if any results are to be expected."

Page 99, paragraph 2: "we must try to repair the damage immediately lest we pay the penalty by a spree."

Page 99, paragraph 3: "it must be on a better basis, since the former did not work."

Page 83, paragraph 1: "Yes, there is a long period of reconstruction ahead. We must take the lead."

Page 83, paragraph 2: "We must remember that ten or twenty years of drunkenness would make a skeptic out of anyone."

Page 74, paragraph 1: "Those of us belonging to a religious denomination which requires confession must, and of course, will want to go to the properly appointed authority whose duty it is to receive it."

Page 74, paragraph 2: "The rule is we must be hard on ourself, but always considerate of others."

Page 75, paragraph 1: "But we must not use this as a mere excuse to postpone."

Page 85, paragraph 3: "But we must go further and that means more action."

Page 85, paragraph 2: "Every day is a day when we must carry the vision of God's will into all of our activities."

Page 85, paragraph 2: "These are thoughts which must go with us constantly."

Page 80, paragraph 1: " If we have obtained permission, have consulted with others, asked God to help and the drastic step is indicated we must not shrink."

Page 14, paragraph 2: "I must turn in all things to the Father of Light who presides over us all."

Page 62, paragraph 3: "Above everything, we alcoholics must be rid of this selfishness. We must, or it kills us!"

Page 144, paragraph 3: "The man must decide for himself."

Page 89, paragraph 2: "To watch people recover, to see them help others, to watch loneliness vanish, to see a fellowship grow up about you, to have a host of friends - this is an experience you must not miss."

Page 33, paragraph 3: "If we are planning to stop drinking, there must be no reservation of any kind."

Page 79, paragraph 2: "We must not shrink at anything."

Page 86, paragraph 2: "But we must be careful not to drift into worry, remorse or morbid reflection, for that would diminish our usefulness to others."

Page 120, paragraph 2: "he must redouble his spiritual activities if he expects to survive."

Page 152, paragraph 2: "I know I must get along without liquor, but how can I?"

Page 95, paragraph 3: "he must decide for himself whether he wants to go on."

Page 159, paragraph 3: "Though they knew they must help other alcoholics if they would remain sober, that motive became secondary."

Page 156, paragraph 3: "Both saw that they must keep spiritually active."

Page 130, paragraph 2: "that is where our work must be done."

Page 82, paragraph 3: "Certainly he must keep sober, for there will be no home if he doesn't."

Page 143, paragraph 2: "he should understand that he must undergo a change of heart"

Page 69, paragraph 4: "Whatever our ideal turns out to be, we must be willing to grow toward it."

Page 69, paragraph 4: "We must be willing to make amends where we have done harm."

Page 44, paragraph 3: "we had to face the fact that we must find a spiritual basis of life - or else."

Page 78, paragraph 3: "We must lose our fear of creditors no matter how far we have to go, for we are liable to drink if we are afraid to face them."

Page 93, paragraph 3: "To be vital, faith must be accompanied by self-sacrifice and unselfish, constructive action."

Page 43, paragraph 4: "His defense must come from a Higher Power."

Page 66, paragraph 4: "We saw that these resentments must be mastered."

Page 146, paragraph 4: "For he knows he must be honest if he would live at all."

Page 73, paragraph 5: "We must be entirely honest with somebody if we expect to live long or happily in this world."

But Remember... "When the man is presented with this volume it is best that no one tell him he must abide by its suggestions." - Page 144, paragraph 3.

APPENDIX III

MEMO FROM GOD....

Effective immediately, please be aware that there are changes YOU need to make in YOUR life. These changes need to be completed in order that I may fulfill My promises to you to grant you peace, joy and happiness in this life. I apologize for any inconvenience, but after all that I am doing, this seems very little to ask of you. I know, I already gave you the 10 Commandments. Keep them. But follow these guidelines, also.

1. QUIT WORRYING---Life has dealt you a blow and all you do is sit and worry. Have you forgotten that I am here to take all your burdens and carry them for you? Or do you just enjoy fretting over every little thing that comes your way?

2. PUT IT ON THE LIST---Something needs to be done or taken care of. Put it on the list. No, not YOUR list. Put it on MY to-do-list. Let ME be the one to take care of the problem. I can't help you until you turn it over to Me. And although My to-do-list is long, I am after all...GOD. I can take care of anything you put into My hands. In fact, if the truth were ever really known, I take care of a lot of things for you that you never even realize.

3. TRUST ME---Once you've given your burdens to Me, quit trying to take them back. Trust in Me. Have the faith that I will take care of all your needs. YOUR problems and your trials. Problems with the kids? Put them on My list. Problem with finances? Put it on My list. Problems with your emotional roller coaster? For My sake, put it on My list. I want to help you. All you have to do is ask.

4. LEAVE IT ALONE---Don't wake up one morning and say, "Well, I'm feeling much stronger now, I think I can handle it from here." Why do you think you are feeling stronger now? It's simple. You gave Me your burdens and I'm taking care of them. I also renew your strength and cover you in my peace. Don't you know that if I give you these problems back, you will be right back where you started? Leave them with Me and forget about them. Just let Me do my job.

5. TALK TO ME---I want you to forget a lot of things. Forget what was making you crazy. Forget the worry and the fretting because you know I'm in control. But there's one thing I pray you never forget. Please, don't forget to talk to Me - OFTEN! I love YOU! I want to hear your voice. I want you to include Me in on the things going on in your life. I want to hear you talk about your friends and family. Prayer is simply you having a conversation with Me. I want to be your dearest friend.

6. HAVE FAITH---I see a lot of things from up here that you can't see from where you are. Have faith in Me that I know what I'm doing. Trust Me; you wouldn't want the view from My eyes. I will continue to care for you, watch over you, and meet your needs. You only have to trust Me. Although I have a much bigger task than you, it seems as if you have so much trouble just doing your simple part. How hard can trust be?

7. SHARE---You were taught to share when you were only two years old. When did you forget? That rule still applies. Share with those who are less fortunate than you. Share your joy with those who need encouragement. Share your laughter with those who haven't heard any in such a long time. Share your tears with those who have forgotten how to cry. Share your faith with those who have none.

8. BE PATIENT--- I managed to fix it so in just one lifetime you could have so many diverse experiences. You grow from a child to an adult, have children, change jobs many times, learn many trades, travel to so many places, meet thousands of people, and experience so much. How can you be so impatient then when it takes Me a little longer than you expect to handle something on My to-do-list? Trust in My timing, for My timing is perfect. Just because I created the entire universe in only six days, everyone thinks I should always rush, rush, rush.

9. BE KIND---Be kind to others, for I love them just as much as I love you. They may not dress like you, or talk like you, or live the same way you do, but I still love you all. Please try to get along, for My sake. I created each of you different in some way. It would be too boring if you were all identical. Please, know I love each of your differences.

10. LOVE YOURSELF---As much as I love you, how can you not love yourself? You were created by me for one reason only -- to be loved, and to love in return. I am a God of Love. **Love Me.** Love your neighbors. But also love yourself. It makes My heart ache when I see you so angry with yourself when things go wrong.

You are very precious to me. Don't ever forget that!

With all My heart I love YOU!   **GOD**
(www.smilegodlovesyou.org)

Bibliography

Dick B   http://www.dickb.com/

Dr. Silkworth   http://www.silkworth.net

A.A. history   http://www.aahistory.com

Smile God Loves You   http://smilegodlovesyou.org

Northwest Arkansas A.A.   http://www.nwarkaa.org

Alcoholics Anonymous. (1939, 1955, 1976, 2001). Alcoholics Anonymous, Alcoholics Anonymous World Services, Inc.

Made in the USA
Lexington, KY
09 December 2012